# THE ADMEN
# MOVE ON
# LHASA

# THE ADMEN MOVE ON LHASA

## WRITING AND CULTURE IN A VIRTUAL WORLD

# STEVEN HEIGHTON

Published in 1997 by
House of Anansi Press Limited
1800 Steeles Avenue West, Concord, ON
Canada  L4K 2P3

*Distributed in Canada by*
General Distribution Services Inc.
30 Lesmill Road
Toronto, Canada  M3B 2T6
Tel. (416) 445-3333
Fax (416) 445-5967
e-mail: Customer.Service@ccmailgw.genpub.com

*Distributed in the United States by*
General Distribution Services Inc.
85 River Rock Drive, Suite 202
Buffalo, New York 14207
Toll free 1-800-805-1083
Fax (416) 445-5967
e-mail: Customer.Service@ccmailgw.genpub.com

01  00  99  98  97    1  2  3  4  5

CATALOGING IN PUBLICATION DATA

Heighton, Steven, 1961–
The admen move on Lhasa : writing and culture in a virtual world

ISBN 0-88784-588-6

1. Title.

PS8565.E451A74 1997   C814'.54   97-930111-4
PR9199.3.H45A67 1997

Cover design: Bill Douglas@The Bang
Printed and bound in Canada
Typesetting: ECW Type & Art, Oakville

*House of Anansi Press gratefully acknowledges the support of the Canada Council and the Ontario Arts Council in the development of writing and publishing in Canada.*

*For Michael Holmes and Jay Ruzesky*

# CONTENTS

To bring the forest primeval inside, USG interiors, the well-known manufacturers of acoustic tile, has created Interior Trees, 19-foot-tall artificial trees made of aluminum and steel.

USG's Merritt Seymour told *Metropolis* magazine that the company's design team had been looking for a product that would be a metaphor for a better life. Trees, which provide shelter and help purify the air, fit the bill. "We wanted to create a product that could contribute positively to a person's well-being, whether it's used in a health-care setting, a restaurant, a mall or an office," Seymour said.

Interior Trees look like a cross between a sun umbrella and a tree. Trunks have electrical outlets, phone hookups and vents for air circulation. The lowest "branches" have lamps; above that are large "palm-like fronds" of micro-perforated steel, says *Metropolis*, "which seem to shift slightly — as the eye travels across them."

The designers visualize the trees standing in large rooms and functioning as spatial anchors. Groups of desks can be clustered around them.

(From the San Francisco *Chronicle*, reprinted
in the *Globe and Mail*, 18 September 1996)


All that is institution and theory ceases to be life.

— E. M. Cioran, *Tears & Saints*


This world is falling, failing,
and we the guilty merchants set to flee.

— Mary Cameron, *Clouds Without Heaven*

*Prologue*

# Deaths and Entrances

*Notes towards a fictional memoir*

A FEW WEEKS AFTER my first book was published, I took part in a bizarre poetry reading in Kingston. It was to be my first public reading and I was terrified. Like the condemned poet trussed in his chair awaiting death in the final scene of the war film *Breaker Morant*, I and two other, older writers sat side by side at the back of a new bookstore facing an audience about the size of a firing squad. Behind them a glass door and plate glass windows framed a rowdy expanse of Princess Street: Saturday afternoon and the street and sidewalks were crammed with duelling honking cars, pods of shoppers, and hordes of Mohawked, face-painted Queen's frosh, drunk and celebrating the end of exams. Some of them stopped and stood tottering at the window, leering in at us, mooning purple faces against the glass. *The peanut-crunching crowd shoves in to see.*

Now, eight years removed, it's hard to figure how I could have seen that small audience of placid book lovers — and in my own city, too — as my jury and executioners, but that day in the bookstore the fear really was debilitating and the presence of two veterans to the right and left of me only made it worse. They sensed my panic and they tried to help — "You need the nerves to read well," one told me, "the trick is to make the butterflies fly in formation" — but clearly they had no idea how tattered my nerves had gotten.

The double rye I'd downed in the back had not yet kicked in.

I began to see it wasn't going to.

Such panic seems hard to fathom now, but then I was reading in public for the first time, and from a new book, a first book, and in the hearing of two well-known, widely praised writers, the shelves around us amply stocked with their achievements. And I wanted so much to shine.

Bronwen Wallace was the first reader that day. When she marvelled, in her poem "Common Magic," at how the mechanic managed to fix the car "through whatever storm he's trapped inside," I felt the irony, I may even have smiled. But then, my own storm sweeping back, I heard little more of what was to be one of her last readings. Nobody knew that then. It must have been a powerful reading because at the end the audience — which had swelled appallingly just before she started and now packed the tiny store — gave out a thunderclap of initial applause and the secondary rumblings went on for some time. Too long, I felt, a hard act to follow; not long enough by half.

The ovation died out. After a few seconds Bronwen Wallace gave me a nudge with her elbow. It was as bad as I'd feared. Worse. I had no control of my voice, the words were lodging in my throat, to the audience I might have seemed a mime executing some macabre performance piece — the blanched diner desperately asphyxiating, amid stran-gled whimpers for help. Then a strange thing began to happen. Heeding the advice of the third writer to *look* at the audience while reading, I braved a quick glance upward and saw above the watching faces — all contorted in pale agonies of politeness — a curious change outside. The chrome-flashes of passing cars had ceased. The people on the street were no longer bustling past but standing at attention, rows of them, darkening the windows — though not looking in. They were facing away, heads swivelled to the left, upstreet. Through gaps in the crowd I caught the gaudy flash of men in dress uniform, marching. My voice faltered. There was music. Bagpipes, unmistakably, and from farther off the lumbering drone of a marching band. The crowd was deepening and a big man in a Queen's Crew jacket stumbled back into the door. As it jarred inward, then swung closed, a breath of fresh air chuffed in with the full blare of the music and the hum and simmer of the crowd.

A limousine convertible cruised into view. The mayor and her husband, with waxen smiles, stood back of the chauffeur, pivoting stiffly and waving like wind-up figurines on a wedding cake. Next came a float looming and shimmering over the heads of the crowd: a small-scale Plexiglass office tower on wheels with a half-dozen men — charcoal suits, briefcases — milling around on the penthouse, waving and beaming like delighted executives in an AmEx ad.

Somehow my voice, feebler than ever, had creaked on through all of this. Heads in the audience kept turning, furtive, towards the street — then politely back towards me. There was a desperate tension in the room. I mumbled on. Then with little warning the second wave of pipers was upon us and I let its shrill tirade swallow the last of my voice.

The veteran writers on either side of me were sitting bolt upright, hands locked in their laps like the buckles of fastened seatbelts. Lips clamped together too. And I could tell they were doing this for me, that they feared I would be shamed and hurt if they broke rank and started laughing a few minutes into my début. But as the pipers sirened on down Princess Street and a new float steamed into sight (it looked like a giant serving of lasagna on wheels — or no, more like moussaka, while the next float was definitely a Greek salad in the midst of whose crêpe greens and vast plastic tomato wedges three moustached restauranteurs stood, toasting the crowds) the other writer, Tom Marshall, let slip one of his nervous chuckles. Bronwen Wallace followed suit with helpless gusto. The marching band was now thundering past us, the leader goose-stepping and twirling a giant Q-tip baton while two flag-bearers followed with a white banner reading KINGSTON & DISTRICT UNITED PHARMACIES. Behind them came a bobbing panoply of costumed dwarves done up as huge, self-propelled Listerine and vitamin C and Buckley's Mixture bottles, a pill box, a lean Neo Citran packet with long perky legs in green tights, a waving lab-coated pharmacist with a massive, Aspirin-shaped Happy Face head.

For a moment I tried to raise my voice over the boozy trombone riffs and the tuba's elephantine farting. No use. I heard myself begin to laugh. The spell was broken and the whole audience cracked up. The only one in the store not yet laughing was the organizer of the event, who stood shaking her lowered head, muttering something about the "Chamber of Commerce parade" and how she had phoned and someone had assured her, *assured* her. . . . But it didn't matter. I felt wonderful and told her so. I felt . . . reprieved, as if the band leader in his scarlet tunic and epaulets had been the officer who comes sprinting towards the execution ground with the order of clemency in his white kid glove.

When it all ended I finished my reading with a stronger voice and a kind of inaugural confidence which has grown in the years since. Grown and faded, grown and faded. But generally grown. Still, I've given up hope that the lingering sense, or fear, of being a chronic apprentice — a burning novice finally ignored by the audience and drowned out by the passing world — will ever fade altogether. For everyone who writes, I think, it's the same.

And after the reading, wine, food. The animated chatter of people who seem to be discussing everything except the event itself, but that's all right, you're relieved and thirsty and there are always a few people with kind words, questions. Now that the actual reading is behind you everything seems so agreeable, genteel, and though that's a relief from the solitude of the writing life, with its compulsory and punishing introspection, abandoned novels, occupational self-doubt (and unshareable small triumphs, that ideal word or detail pinned down), a part of you knows that the wine and cheese and the book table and the trade talk and the gossip and the beaming civility have nothing to do with the real work. Some readings and parties are a brief reprieve, a way to balance the loneliness, while others just seem to mock it.

Before Bronwen Wallace and Tom Marshall died, still young, they were focal points for the Kingston literary community — the kind of writers who throw parties, attend readings, edit anthologies, encourage new writers on the scene; the kind of ardent activists without whom there is no scene. Bronwen Wallace died of cancer in the summer of 1989, in a circle of friends, while Tom Marshall died alone, suddenly, of a heart attack, in 1993.

Sometimes when I think about them and those times, I think also of the young Toronto writer/editor Daniel Jones, who took his own life in the winter of 1994. Not that the three of them had much in common as writers, or even as people; Daniel Jones, at least in his last few years, rarely went to parties, readings, public functions of any kind. But he did go to the AGM of the Writers' Union of Canada (the first and last one he attended, I think) which took place in Kingston soon after that strange sideshow of a reading. I met him there. He was the first writer from outside the Kingston area to tell me he'd read my book. Though he wasn't much older than I was, he seemed to me widely published, well known, a "name writer," like Tom and Bronwen — and, again like them, he encouraged me when I needed it most.

So now when I think of the deaths of those writers, all of them generous to me and the many new voices they praised or mentored or edited, I tend to confuse and conflate events so it almost seems as if Daniel Jones could have been present at that reading of ours, my comic initiation. I wish he had been. I think he would have relished the irony of that collision between worlds and laughed as the others laughed at that comic strip unreeling past us, frame by frame, the Real World too busy and beleaguered for poetry — a world whose antic, undeviating bustle betrays the charade, the clown-masked panic, the truth that the secular parade is more funeral march than triumphal procession. Always crashing past, indifferent. And inside the circle of art's communal isolation, the more poignant quarantine of the individual writer afraid even of the "converted"; afraid of *their* indifference, since such a thing would leave nowhere else to go.

Afraid of their scorn.

Too late now to join the parade.

And many of those who feel as you do are vanishing.

# I

# The Admen Move on Lhasa

*Modern society is held together by fear.*
— Václav Havel

IF THERE ARE CITIES in the world that seem like works of art — Bacchic odes, abstract paintings, huge novels, vulgar and vibrant, or elaborate, classical symphonies — it's not only because of their overt beauty but because of some inner dynamism and complexity, a diverse yet somehow unified richness. I want to go back to Lhasa even now. Lhasa, Tibet, is, or was, a living and visionary place which until recently showed how a city could be a lasting work of art — the kind that continues to glow on the map that every curious mind contains, or on the pulsing globe a traveller's heart becomes over time; the kind that remains in the heart as both a consolation and abiding challenge. Or an invitation: Let death come at the end of life, not the middle or the start. What all art finally means.

Whatever means less than that, it seems to me, is just advertising or schlock.

Yet this is an age and a place where nothing is meant to mean anything at all and it's seen as somehow rustic and rhinocerine to believe in the possibility of real significance; addicted to both irrelevance and irreverence we come to sound in our discourse and conversation more and more like extras on the set of a Hollywood film or a TV ad, while our cities more and more resemble the set itself. If the Kingston writer Kent Nussey is right to revise Oscar Wilde's famous dictum by arguing that these days life imitates journalism, not art, it seems to me that you could fairly substitute for "journalism" the words advertising, or schlock. I'm nostalgic and no doubt a bit poetic and naïve when it comes to Lhasa and places like it, not only because they're about to disappear, but because I see and feel how far our own cities and our own art fall short of the visionary standards set by doomed worlds like Lhasa, or Nepal, or precolonial Tahiti. Places where the primary life-impulse, imperfectly honoured or not, was a will to celebration, gratitude, and reverence, not to confiscation and control.

Of course the characteristic (and spiritually crippling) *ir*reverence and irony of today are necessary adaptations, a psychic camouflage evolved for use in a technojungle ruled by admen, fibre opticians, schlockmongers, and CEOs; yet the layers that protect us also smother us, weigh us down. I want to find my way out of this electronic chain mail and back up into the sheer, high, unwired air of Lhasa, and soon — but lacking the time and the plane ticket and knowing at any rate that the place is now changed, changed utterly, I'll have to go back in words.

If the primary life-impulse in our society is a will to confiscation and control, it's bound to get into our art; although the best writers do tend to work in reaction against the dominant trends of their time, they have to breathe the same toxic air as everybody else — and what is a poem, finally, but life-breath exhaled and given form? Inevitably much Western writing is marred by this atmospheric will to control, or by the human will itself, which does and must play a role in the creation of any art, but not the executive role to which it's too often promoted.*

It's as if our world has become a kind of schlock film punctuated by threatening advertisements, so that writers have to struggle more than ever to remain artists, true to a calling, and not be turned into advertisers, with mere careers. And somehow still feed the kids. I say these things in full knowledge of the new academic orthodoxy that holds there's no way to distinguish, finally, between advertising and art, or between schlock and art, or art and other things. But I think there is; and the controlling writer who tries to manage the reader and regulate too closely his or her passage through the avenues and back alleys of a book is en route to becoming a kind of advertiser or schlockster instead of an artist — or, to put it differently, the kind of tour guide who's always trying to usher his charges into a cousin's souvenir shop or an uncle's café.

Consider the Nobel laureates Pearl S. Buck and John Steinbeck, whose reputations have suffered a steady erosion over the last few decades largely because the manipulative sentimentality and didacticism of books like *The Good Earth* and *The Grapes of Wrath* have grown manifest as the ideological dust blurring those defects has thinned and cleared. *The Grapes of Wrath* is a big-hearted, sometimes brilliant

---

* The new electronic technologies that facilitate the process of literary creation tend to give a writer an illusory sense of control, or will to control, over materials which have or should be granted a certain life of their own. Clearly such advances, though useful, will extend or exacerbate our existing preoccupations with control, our fear of natural process.

book, and it's impossible for readers of an egalitarian temper not to be swept up by the spirit of humane, anticorporate solidarity running through it; but reconsidering the book now it becomes clear that the dust swirling through the desiccated plains of the Great Depression was not only sanding away dreams and lives and ways of life, but, for Steinbeck's purposes at least, throwing up a kind of smoke-screen behind which an advertiser or a tour guide was at work.

Yet the book did have an important social effect in its time. So perhaps Steinbeck, by doing a good sales job on the decent principles he believed in, sacrificed aesthetic lon-gevity for the sake of social change. For even when the customer is satisfied with the product, a kind of subtle, underground resentment begins to smoulder inside anyone who has been talked into something. There is an anarchist in every heart that would rather discover and embrace things of its own free will — and in the act of embracing, suffuse the discovery with something of itself, thus making it, at least partly, its own. So the serendipitous traveller who happens on a city which hasn't (as yet) been hyped in any guidebook or tourist brochure will come to love it and hold its memory far longer than the package tourist will remember, say, the Lhasa of 1997, where one is no longer free to explore at will. But the Lhasa of only a decade back: an open book, a richly illuminated, multitudinous conclave of poems, not a Cham-ber of Commerce brochure, not a catalogue.

Obviously Steinbeck was not the only writer who used his work as a vehicle for ideas (not unlike a Dust Bowl travelling salesman transporting his wares over the Great Plains in a creaking old Chevy). By the late thirties Bertolt Brecht believed his age and milieu to be so wretched and beset that simply to write of trees was "a kind of crime" because there were so many other, more pressing matters to explore, or attack. And W. H. Auden wrote that poets were sometimes faced with social predicaments so urgent that to write of anything else would be to fail in one's fundamental human duties — though artists in that situation had to accept that by subserving their work to conscious, specific political ends and selling a cause, no matter how valid, they were betraying and diminishing the cause of art: an act of necessary evil.

But most of the time such acts are unnecessary. The moral orientation of artists to the world — their "politics" — is the bedrock of everything they create and will always exert an underground influence on the lay of the land, its visible contours. Morality in art is tectonic, not the work of back-hoes and bulldozers, but the Human Will Inc. will always prefer to square things away or to spell everything out — and through a bullhorn if possible — like a crowd-control cop or a clearance-house huckster. Willfully political (as opposed to integrally political) fiction and poetry betray an elitist lack of faith in the reader, and sometimes expose authors so uncertain of their own convictions, or afraid of what those convictions might turn out to be if given leave to emerge uncontrolled, that the writers resort to propaganda, to the act of protesting too much.

No matter how important (and with notable exceptions, such as the protest songs of Leadbelly or Bob Dylan, the films of Eisenstein, the plays of Brecht) overtly ideological work is less than art because it's a form of advertising instead — and here arises the theoretical objection I referred to earlier. Terry Eagleton and other important critical theorists would counter that art forms cannot be ranked, that "art" per se is not finally distinguishable from things traditionally seen as nonart or as pseudo-art — a sample of graffiti, say, or a postered ad in a subway. (Or the kind of work I've just mentioned, that sets itself up as art but on some levels is a form of advertising.) Eagleton's argument is complex and compelling and witty but it fails to account for one crucial distinction: while some graffiti clearly *is* art, most advertising, whether overt or disguised as a novel, is not, the essential difference being that art usually involves an invitation and solicits the entry and collaboration of the audience, while advertising usually implies a threat. Or, to continue this meandering trip towards Lhasa: art invites you into the city along any available road, while advertising dictates where you enter. And when.

If Lhasa or the livelier parts of Toronto suggest the city as baroque, carnivalesque art form, then Bay Street and Bramalea represent the city as TV ad — John Newlove's "cold soul of [a] city blown empty by commerce."

It's not that art should be apolitical, or ever can be, but that politics, in art, should be apropagandist.

Art makes you a full citizen. Advertising makes you a subject.

If a poetry book is a country or a city, then think of the book's opening poem as a lopsided, not quite legible sign at a fork in the road. The fork is at times a triple, a quadruple split, and the route is ambiguous, the road often rough. Or see the poem instead as a sign at the entrance to a city, a town —

WELC ME TO NOR H BO RN  R VER
pop lat n

— a sign whose mere existence, in this barren place, asserts human welcome, but whose words can't quite be read. What city is this? What town? Nothing for it but to explore. The "population" can't quite be made out either; you'll have to encounter and tally up the inhabitants firsthand.

And an advertisement? A road sign at another fork: a sign indicating unequivocally the one right route and implying the possibility of some misfortune if the directions are ignored. (DOGS MUST BE CARRIED ON THE ESCALATOR is Eagleton's example of a sign which, by virtue of its "ambiguity" and rich linguistic potential, can be read as a poem. The argument is ingenious and entertaining but finally a bit cranked up; in context, passersby know what the sign means, and recognize the threat implied in the imperative "must.")

Invitation as opposed to coercion: the difference between art and advertising is like the difference between a city that attracts and invites you by reputation, then by sight (in the distance, drawing near along any number of roads) — and a theme park, or that planned capital whose layout obliges you to follow a set route in (and which, monolithic, grey and lifeless as a cenotaph, repels you anyway). It's natural and poignantly human for writers to want to evoke certain responses in readers and to avoid others — critical scorn, for example — but in the end the desire to regulate and control readers and tour-guide them in to the stiff, central, ministerial edifice of a MORAL or a MESSAGE is self-destructive — and as doomed to frustration as the desire to regulate gossip and opinion about oneself. Oscar Wilde wisely lived "in perpetual fear of not being misunderstood"; a writer too fearful of *being* misunderstood resembles the architect of that planned and lifeless modern metropolis primarily accessed by way of an efficient, well-lit and signposted eight-lane cloverleafed collector-laned superhighway. YIELD TO ONCOMING TRAFFIC. NO LEFT TURN ALLOWED.

More snippets of critical theory lyric to shame Sappho into silence.

RIGHT LANE MUST EXIT.

It works, in a way, this system of hardened arteries, and

initially commuters will be impressed by the megalithic grandeur and high-tech efficiency of the apparatus. But years later, looking back on their visit to the metropolis, the place will recur to them with little vividness or lustre because the approach to a city indelibly colours the filled-out, final impression. (The endless prefab franchise strip on the highway into Santa Fe actually makes the handsome old adobe plaza at the centre seem faintly ersatz, as if it were all a false front, a movie set, a setup.)

Better to invite the reading commuter into a city which, like Lhasa — even the McModernized Lhasa of 1997 — can be approached from many directions and in many ways: by foot along pilgrim tracks, by shuddering bus or truck over the highway in from Golmud or on the unpaved mountain road from Kathmandu, by horse cart over the desert — or by antiquated commuter jet, on China's international airline, CA, whose advertising and motto really ought to run

CHINA AIR LINES:

WHY NOT

PUT YOUR LIFE

IN *OUR* HANDS

As with any work of art worth the viewing, it takes effort to get to Lhasa, and there are dangers along the way. The city is on a dry plateau 11,000 feet above the level of the nearest sea — the Bay of Bengal a thousand miles to the south — and is rimmed-in by a circle of treeless, bone-coloured peaks like the sides and fingers of a vast, cupped hand. In the palm of which the city lies. To land at Lhasa's airstrip the jet must clear the sides of the Buddha's vast hand and then nosedive at a terrifying stunt-plane angle so that many of the passengers, already pale and shaken after three hours in the friendly skies with CA (CHINA AIR LINES: WHERE

THE PILOTS ARE THE TERRORISTS), actually cry out in fear, a communal gasp rushing down the aisle and mounting to a shriek as the craft seems to freefall into a spin. (It happened that our flight was passing through a Himalayan storm just then and a perfectly timed, apocalyptic crump of thunder sundered the clouds at the moment we commenced our plunge into the abyss. It should be noted too that three hours earlier the confidence of the few tourists on board had been severely tested by the following brief announcement: "Welcome to China Air Lines. We will be flying at an altitude of approximately three feet for the next thirty-two thousand hours. Thank you for your English.")

But you do land and when you emerge into the searching light and that shrill, crystal air censered with burning juniper and ripening barley you know you're in a world far more real than the "Real World" of Western commerce and "responsibility" and at the heart of an ancient culture still showing unmistakable life signs. Which is to say: a place where you might still believe, however partially or briefly, that the gods are not all dead and their unmarked graves paved over on the franchise-fringes of town.

Say it's the dizzying thinness of the air. It could well be. But that heady sense of arrival in an unfamiliar, exquisitely disturbing place — surely that is the feeling that living art gives us as we're airlifted into the heart of it or drive in through its outer bounds. At the same time there's a sense of the familiar, and even the familial — a sense of coming home — but always quickened, leavened with strangeness.

Perhaps artists can begin to suspect they've created a memorable city, a god-haunted world or a visionary town — some site worthy of repeated pilgrimage — only when responses to the work are unpredictably and ungovernably divergent, diverse, off the wall, missing the point that good artists do sometimes try to make but without ever quite succeeding — always seeming instead to convey something else. Something broader, more manifold. Something impossible to signpost.

The danger to a modern writer consists in the desire — arising from the urban-industrial will to control, now so empowered by technology, and from the universal human fear of censure and misunderstanding — to update the fabulous Lhasa that every good poem or story tends towards, to force it online, to fasten a grid over its organic sprawlings and meanderings, and to mark too clearly a lone superhighway in. Or a franchise strip. The muse crucified on golden arches. (The mayor of North York blueprinting and building a "downtown" for his suburban borough instead of letting a centre, a city heart, develop on its own — if it had to. That brain-built city heart standing empty after rush hour, empty and forgotten, as the artifacts of the will are always forgotten in the end.)

En route to a more reverent and organic place, Lhasa, I come to believe Eagleton and the theorists are wrong: it's not stuffy, elitist, and impossible to distinguish between art and "lower things," like advertising and schlock. The old authentic Lhasa, god-haunted and culturally unique, a law unto itself, does represent the city as art form, while much of the new Lhasa — like the prefab franchise strip on the outskirts of Santa Fe — is schlock. And, like all schlock, it's punctuated by advertisements: billboard after billboard, larger than life, pixel-blinking its clandestine threats over the freeway into the unreal city. Drink Polar Beer and you will be part of a loving huddle of glamorous triathletes; don't drink it and you will, by implication or more direct visual cue, languish in solitude as one of the ostracized, a geeky exile from the affable tribe. Fail to use ReekEnd deodorant (WHY BE THE DEATH OF THE PARTY? REEKEND FOR A BETTER WEEKEND!) or Gargoyle Mouthwash (GARGLE WITH GARGOYLE! LET THE GARGOYLE GARGOYLE KEEP YOUR MOUTH FRESH!) and you will surely be cast into that same lepers' limbo, that ghetto of untouchables. Smoke Kit Carcin King-Size and resemble a rancher or a vigilante, stubble-chinned, armed, autonomous, invulnerable. And the alternatives?

Art doesn't try to sell anything or to make threats. In some of his Cantos, Pound, with the irascible ardour of an Old Testament prophet, tries to sell us his ideology of anti-Semitism by making millennial predictions and maledictions and threats. Choked into silence by the sulphurous fumes of his wrath, Pound's muse, it would seem, has made for the door. What is left is a bale of tendentious, manipulative, and bullying screeds — as much advertising as art.*

And schlock? I've set it up as the opposite of art, but seeing as I've also cast advertising in that role it might seem as though I see schlock and advertising as equivalent. But schlock — mindless, formulaic, manipulative TV and movie entertainment of all kinds — is very different from advertising, in fact almost its opposite, although the two forms do coexist in a highly effective symbiosis. In Jungian terms, advertising is schlock's shadow. For while advertising

---

* Or even a kind of propaganda. Propaganda, which in its crudest forms can be recognized easily by the fulsome use of exclamation marks, does not invite the reader's agreement, as a good essay should do, but seeks instead to coerce and exact it. In the statements SMASH THE STATE! or IMMIGRANTS OUT! the exclamation marks function as visual truncheons which the propagandist employs to deliver coercive psychic blows on the consciousness of the reader.

threatens, schlock appeases and sedates, in a constant cycle that keeps denizens of the unreal city at once docile and in a panic of desire — desire for all the secular baubles and buyables and not the internal riches of that higher city Rilke has in mind in issuing his famous invitation, or warning — almost, but in context not quite, a threat — *You must change your life.*

Schlock is not art precisely because of the way it works to prevent such life-change from happening. Schlock, because it works to perpetuate psychic and physical inertia as opposed to growth, is on the side of death, not life. Schlock is any species of entertainment that facilitates the demi-life of the drugged consumer, as it does by offering vicarious thrills that temporarily vent the pressure we sometimes feel, from our own souls, to start living more fully. Schlock is a quick fix that buys the devil more time. Schlock preempts, bit by bit, our higher passions — the will to freedom, beauty, empathy, love — until finally the will to change dwindles and nothing is left but the compulsion to acquire and collect and consume. Schlock suborns us into living through champions (in the old sense of the word) rather than striving to become the heroes of our own lives; each visiting team the Leafs vanquish, every straw man that Rambo blows away is one of our own demons, dead, and without our having raised a hand. But not quite dead. Stunned, and soon to waken. More ravenous than ever; hungry for the next game, or for *Rambo* vii.

Schlock makes us understudies loitering in the wings of our own lives.

Of course by this definition many things that would presume to be seen as art — like *Schindler's List*, with its reassuringly one-dimensional view of evil — are really schlock. It's not that art cannot be entertainment, the way schlock is, or is advertised to be, but rather that art, while entertaining us, also unsettles. For whatever sedates us is shuffling us off towards the greater sleep of death. Art, on the other hand, is a persistent wake-up call, the setting off of a quiet siren in the heart. (Standing on the cliffs above the Sky Burial site near Lhasa, where the dead, ritually dismembered, are returned to the air by mountain birds who carry off their remains, I scrawled in my notebook *This country is an invitation to receive the wind*. And now it seems to me that art is the same thing. Art is an invitation to change what can be changed — one's self, first and finally — and to cherish what is receding, vanishing, as all things are.)

And schlock? Like advertising, it urges us to believe that some things can be made not to vanish, can be made to last forever — and, like the tour guide's Lhasa, they can be owned and consumed. And that the act of consumption and the condition of ownership form a kind of double expressway into the city of happiness. The only way in. So in this sense at least they're on the same road as that failed art that seeks to guide us in to the warehouse and its one, unequivocal, transredemptive point.

I want, very much, to go back to Lhasa. On the rare occasions when I encounter people who've recently made the trip, I pull them aside with the neurotic urgency of an ancient mariner and ask for the latest details. Inevitably they recount, with the animated, almost nostalgic horror of the survivor, the flight in. Eventually they tell me about the city and the new Tibet. Most of them depict a marvellous place, as Lhasa must be still, no doubt, but more and more their travelogues feature alarming details: the old traditional travellers' inns (where tourists could actually meet and speak with Tibetans) closed down and replaced by a monolithic Holiday Inn and other state-controlled chain hotels where all tourists are duly herded; overland journeys to the capital increasingly restricted, so that CA's senile fleet is virtually the sole way in; McDonald's, of course, their malignant clown-mascot more and more a kind of universal ambassador for phony food and enfeebling pseudo-nutrition.

One traveller told me how she and her husband, trying to enter a traditional Tibetan noodle shop, were stopped by a Chinese soldier and led away. He was friendly and gentle enough, the soldier, but insistent, and clear in his directives. The noodle shop was off-bounds. Please, he said, guiding them towards the new part of town, this way a little. Please. Over there — you see? — over there is a place you could dine.

# 2

# Elegy in Stone

## *Vimy Ridge, April 1992*

THE PARK'S ENTRANCE — a border crossing, really — was modest enough: a small sign you could easily miss if you were driving past. But we were on foot. And though it turned out to be a much longer walk than we'd expected, it was a good place to walk, the fields along the road billowing with mustard, wheat, and poppies, the oaks and maples fragrant with new growth. We could be in Canada, I thought — then remembered that, for official purposes, we were.

The wind as we neared the ridge grew chilly, the sky grey.

Before long the road passed through a forest of natural growth and entered an old plantation of white pines, thick and towering, a spacious colonnade receding in the gloom. Fences appeared along the road, then signs warning us not to walk among the trees where sheep foraged above grassed-in trenches, shell holes, unexploded mines. In the blue-green, stained-glass light of the forest, the near-silence was eerie, solemn, as in the cathedral at Arras.

Finally we heard voices, saw a file of parked cars ahead through the trees and came out at the main exhibit site of the park, some distance below the monument that crowns Vimy Ridge. Here, in 1917, from a line of trenches now preserved in concrete and filled daily with French tourists, the Canadian troops had launched their attack. Preserved likewise is the first obstacle they had met: the front-line German trench, barely a grenade's throw away. This whites-of-their-eyes proximity surprised us and made stories of verbal fraternization between the lines — of back and forth banter in broken English and German — all the more plausible, and poignant.

A few years after the end of the First World War the government of France gave Canada a sizeable chunk of the cratered, barren terrain around Vimy Ridge, where 20,000 Canadians fell before the ridge was finally taken on 12 April 1917. Today many Canadian visitors to France pass the memorial park en route to Arras or Lille without realizing the site is officially a small piece of Canada. Though "plot" might be a better word, for although the trenches where Canadian and Allied soldiers lived and died during their siege have healed over, the fields are scarred with cemeteries and the woodlots filled with unmarked graves.

We'd arrived the night before in nearby Arras, finding a hotel and visiting the town's medieval cathedral. The hotel manager had elaborately regretted that we hadn't come two weeks earlier, on Easter Monday, when French President François Mitterand and Prime Minister Brian Mulroney and a handful of Vimy veterans had arrived for the seventy-fifth anniversary of the ridge's fall. I told the manager that I'd read about the ceremony back home, but felt the park was probably best experienced without the crowds and fanfare of an official visit. I could have said more but didn't trust my French enough to try explaining how disturbed I'd been by photographs of those heads of state and their aides beaming glibly among the hunched veterans, whose nation-building sacrifice was clearly far from the politicians' minds.

*Nation-building sacrifice* sounds far too much like the kind of pious, pushy rhetoric I've learned to mistrust and fear, yet for years the bloody achievement of the Canadians on Vimy Ridge did stand, like the ridge itself, as a landmark, a high point around which the idea of a distinct Canadian identity could form.

"*C'est magnifique*," the manager told us when we explained we wanted to go. "*Magnifique*."

At the park's main exhibit site we went into a small, undistinguished brick building to see about a tour of the tunnel system under the trenches. The young guides, in Parks Canada uniforms, explained that we'd just missed the tour and unfortunately would have to wait for the next. But as we turned and went outside to confer, they must have noticed the small Canadian flag sewn onto my backpack, because one of them came out after us and beckoned us toward the tunnels. "You should have told us you're Canadian," he said with a soft Manitoba-French accent. "We don't get all that many."

The low-ceilinged, labyrinthine "subways" — where men ate and slept before the attack and couriers ran with their messages and sappers set charges under the German lines — have been carefully restored, but more or less unembellished. The impression, as above in the trenches, was sobering. I was relieved that this sad, clammy underworld had not been brightened up into some gaudy monument to Our Glorious Past; I was relieved that it still looked, and felt, like a tomb. It reminded me of the tunnels of the besieged Huguenots under the cathedral in Arras.

It was good to get back up into the daylight. We agreed to meet Mario and the other guides for a beer that night in town.

We followed the road up the last part of the ridge to the monument, wind blowing over the bare fields in a steady barrage. Seventy-five years before, the Canadians had advanced at dawn through driving sleet and snow, and now, nearing the exposed crown of the ridge, we could see how weather of that intensity must be quite common. The monument stands atop Hill 145, the Canadians' final objective and the highest point for miles around — but on the morning of the attack it must have been invisible through the snow and the timed barrage behind which the men were advancing.

Before the hilltop and the monument came in sight I'd felt uneasy, recalling the many monuments I had seen that stylized or made over the true face of war so as to safeguard an ideology, to comply with aesthetic conventions, or to make life easier for the recruiters of future wars. But as we neared the monument — two enormous white limestone pillars that meet at the base to form a kind of elongated U — I was impressed. And, as before, relieved. I'd first become anxious when the hotel keeper had told us to expect something "magnifique," but now I saw that in a sense he was right, for here was something magnificent in its simplicity, its solemnity, its understatement. And brilliant in its implication, because the pillars did not quite form a triumphant V, as you might expect, but a shape uncannily resembling the sights mounted on machine guns of the First World War — the kind that claimed tens of thousands of Canadian lives in the war and several thousand on the morning of the attack.

I don't believe such resemblances can be assigned to chance. An artist's hand is always guided in large part by the subconscious. I don't know whether the architect of the Vimy monument was ever asked about his intentions, conscious or subconscious, but in a sense they're no longer the point; unlike so many other old monuments, Walter Seymour Allward's is strikingly modern because of the way it surpasses, or second-guesses, all conventional intent.

We drew closer. Our feeling that this monolith was more a cenotaph, a vast elegy in stone instead of petrified hot air, grew stronger. And with it a feeling of pride. But a kind of pride very different, I think, from the tribal, intolerant swagger so many monuments have been built to inspire. A shy pride in our country's awkwardness at blowing its own horn — because sooner or later every country that does blow its own horn, with flamboyance, starts looking for somebody else to outblow. A pride in our reluctance — our seeming inability — to canonize brave, scared, betrayed adolescents as bearded heroes of mythic dimension, larger than life. Unreal.

And the monument is a cenotaph: we find its base inscribed with the names of the 11,285 Canadians whose final resting place is unknown. Blown to pieces. Lost in the mud, or buried anonymously in the graveyards below the ridge. The parade of names marches on and on, a kind of elegy whose heartbreaking syllables are English- and French-Canadian, Ojibway, Ukrainian, Dutch, German, Italian, Japanese . . .

Many are the names of our own distant relations.

The figures carved on and around the monument, though dated in style, are not blowing trumpets or beating breasts or drums. They seem instead to grieve. We round the monument and the Douai Plain fans out below us: another figure, much larger, cloaked, stands apart at the edge of the monument overlooking the plain. Behind her a sparely worded inscription, in English and French, tells of the ridge's fall.

The figure, we will learn later that night, is Canada, "mourning her lost sons."

Tonight in Arras we'll learn other things as well from the Canadian guides we meet for a beer. That the whole park is planted with shrubs and trees from Canada. That 11,285 pines were planted after the war for every lost man whose name appears on the monument. That the prime minister's Easter visit was indeed a grand and lavish affair — everything the monument itself is not — but that the old soldiers on display carried themselves with dignity and a quiet, inconspicuous pride. And it's that feeling we end up coming back to towards the end of the night when the drinks have made us a bit more open and, I suppose, sentimental. Because we learn that these young expatriates have all felt just as we have about the austerity of the Vimy monument — and, by implication, the Canadian tendency to downplay the "heroism" of our achievements, to refuse to idealize, poeticize, and thus censor an obscene, man-made reality.

Or am I wrong to offer Canada these drunken toasts on a virtue that's largely a matter of historical and political necessity? Perhaps what I'm trying to say is that Canadians are lucky to have been spared, so far, that sense of collective power combined with intense tribal identity that makes every imperial nation so arrogant, competitive, and brutal. And as our friends guide us back to our hotel, I wonder if Canadians will ever stop berating themselves for not believing — as too many other nations have believed, and keep on believing — that they're better than others, that they're the chosen, the elect, the Greatest Nation on Earth, with God on their side.

"Make sure to let people back home know about the memorial," Mario calls out as we enter our hotel. And I reflect that a visit to the monument and the many battlefields around it might help convince some Canadians that there are worse things than uncertainty and understatement.

And if the monument doesn't convince them, or the battle-fields, then surely the graveyards will. In the park or within walking distance lie thirty cemeteries where the remains of over 7,000 Canadians are buried. They are peaceful places, conscientiously tended. Flowers bloom over every grave. Many are poppies. The paint on the crosses is fresh, a dazzling white in the April sun. Here, no doubt, many of the boys whose names appear on the monument are actually buried, beneath long files of anonymous crosses, or stones ranked like chairs in a vast, deserted cathedral. Another endless parade, this time of the nameless — though here and there we do find stones inscribed with a name, an age. David Mahon, 1901–1917. IN MEMORY OF OUR DEAR AND ONLY CHILD.

We recite the words aloud, but this time the feeling they inspire has little to do with pride. The huge limestone gunsight looms above us on the ridge as we enter yet another aisle, and read, yet again:

A SOLDIER OF THE GREAT WAR

*A Canadian Regiment*

*Known Unto God*

# 3

# Horse & Train

MOST OF THE BRIEF QUESTION PERIODS that follow public readings of fiction or poetry are polite, easygoing exchanges, the questions affable and unsurprising, but sooner or later any writer who gives readings is faced with questions of a different kind — the kind that no simple answer will address, the kind that forces a writer to reconsider his or her work in a harsh and exacting new light. I've faced such fiercely illuminating questions at several readings now, most recently in Toronto where a man who looked as if he might be a veteran of the Second World War wanted to know why machine guns kept showing up in my work.

I sensed there was no way I could answer the question coherently and completely in the time remaining, because my answer, I saw, would have far less to do with the small world of my writings than with the boundless real world they grew out of — so I promised to talk to the man privately after the reading.

He slipped away before I could.

I wanted to tell him that I think machine guns have pushed their way into several things I've written because — on an intellectual level apart from my fiction and poetry but often affecting it — I've come to see them as richly symbolic of the industrialized world's material "progress" this century. I see the machine gun this way partly because of its emergence as a real military and political force at the century's start (a chronological coincidence of obvious symbolic force), because of its mechanical sophistication, and, most importantly, because its blind, brute, lethal efficiency and depersonalizing power confirm it as a forebear of the dehumanized, faceless culture we live and write in as the century ends.

As the millennium ends.

The machine gun represents the penultimate stage in a process of abstraction that has allowed some four generations of soldier-technicians to kill strangers they cannot even see. (Missiles and nuclear warheads and "smart bombs," of course, represent the ultimate stage.) Early human conflict was a face to face, hands-on affair. Gradually weapons were developed which allowed combatants to kill at some distance, but enemies were never so far apart that they weren't forced to stare each other in the face. Even after the appearance of firearms, soldiers were forced by the crudity of their weapons to hold their fire until they could "see the whites of their [enemies'] eyes" — and the carnage they were so concretely inflicting. The development of rifled gunbarrels allowed soldiers to kill from a greater remove, both physical and emotional, but the victims were still visible, still clearly men. Or, increasingly, women. Children. Little wonder that studies conducted during the First World War showed that eighty percent of the men in the trenches were not even firing at the enemy, with whom, after all, they'd been allowed to fraternize at Christmas and Easter. These statistics, along with the testimony of soldiers after the war, suggest that most men are at best reluctant killers — that there's something

about the human face and form, visible before you, that makes
it hard to pull a trigger. Even today U.S. Marine recruits
and Canadian paratroopers undergo drills involving violent
chants that they repeat day-in day-out in a brainwashing
rhythm — a kind of brutalizing mantra — to overcome all
the internalized taboos against homicide. And still during
the Vietnam War the officers could not coax the firing rate
of their platoons much over forty-five percent.*

But there were machine guns to take up the slack. A
godsend. A solution not quite final but good enough. Which
is how the Great War's more progressive generals, years
before Vietnam, must have seen their new implements as
they rattled out a death knell for the old face to face manner
of fighting. As their factory-new weapons reduced approaching lines of faces to abstract figures, ciphers, a long, bobbing
file of zeroes that could be swept quickly from the ledger.
The machine gunner was trained not to aim through his
gunsight at a single man but to sweep his weapon in a wide
arc over the battlefield, back and forth, so he could see only
blurred faces, blurred figures moving over the field like
digits on a spreadsheet, or vague shapes on the screen of a
video game. The ancient aversion to homicide — partly
intrinsic, partly instilled — was shot to pieces at fifty rounds
a second, effectively destroyed. The development of increasingly long-range artillery and then aircraft capable of bombing
and then, finally, long-range missiles, was an extension of
this movement into abstract mass murder and away from
the cold, concrete, troubling fact of a stranger dying before
your eyes.

---

* Probably — sadly — we should assume that some proportion of the
men who held their fire were simply paralyzed by fear, not restrained
by a sense of humanity.

With almost every war in this century the proportion of civilian to military deaths has risen; surely the reason for this change is not only the indiscriminate nature of firebombs and napalm canisters and machine guns but also the way that men deploying such weapons can no longer feel as responsible or accountable for their actions. It's no harder in the end to murder an "enemy" child whose suffering you'll never see, or know about, than to murder an unseen enemy conscript.

Modern wars stand in the same relation to ancient wars as murder in the first degree stands to manslaughter. Both are crimes, no doubt, but one is a crime of passion while the other, at least partly, is a crime of the scheming, inventive brain.

With malice aforethought.

I would have told the man at the reading something else as well: that machine guns and literature have far more to do with each other than you might think, that one of the reasons I cherish good writing is that it sets up a concrete human counterpoise to the abstract impersonality and inhuman efficiency of the machine gun, the nuclear warhead, the smart bomb. And, for that matter, the assembly line, the shopping mall, the burgeoning, rigidifying state. Poetry and fiction — especially when the writing is sensuous and visceral instead of cerebral, abstract — are deeply rehumanizing and for that reason they're subversive, whether overtly political or not. Art, and literature above all, is uniquely equipped to convey that indispensible facility, that rare and socially redemptive force, the habit of empathy — of trying to see through the eyes of others and to feel with another's body and heart. I think of literature as putting us face to face — and, at times, hand to hand, in struggle or in love — with strangers. So we're forced to look them in the eyes and see them not as others but as variations on a vast, familiar theme. Ourselves.

If the slaughtered on the battlefields and the doorsteps of Vimy, Dieppe, Tibet, Khe Sanh, East Timor, or Soweto are the flesh made number, digitized, then the characters of a Wilfred Owen war poem, or a Pat Barker or Ninh Bao novel, are the flesh made word, made actual. Or, as Roy Campbell put it in the lines that inspired one of Alex Colville's best-known paintings:

> Against a regiment I oppose a brain
> And a dark horse against an armoured train.

I wish Campbell hadn't had to find a rhyme, because I think "heart" would have been a more worthy, if less precise, noun than "brain." It's a brilliant couplet, but Campbell's choice of word betrays a Victorian confidence in the intellect which strikes me as naïve and out of place in a century where the brain — uncoupled from the grounding, counterbalancing heart — has proved itself a smart bomb.

# 4

# Training for the Millennium

I MIGHT HAVE BEEN A RUNNER. Maybe, if I hadn't been
ambushed by language, or even if I had but had still chosen
a different kind of life: simpler, more robust, a life lived
more in the bones and the blood and the solar plexus, less
in the skull. Since the ones who do live and work solely in
that office of bone spend their lives peering out at the world
through the eye sockets of their own *memento mori*, like
those monks who sleep in coffins "to remind them of their
last end."

Actually I was a runner, back in high school, where I chose
running because it was the only sport I was cut out for. I
suppose I might have stuck with it instead of simply coming
back to it now, fifteen years later, when it's too late to get
really serious. Sometimes I wish I had.

It was back at the same high school I first encountered
the idea that "ontogeny recapitulates phylogeny" — that
the development of the embryo and fetus reconfigures the
evolution of the race — and it occurs to me now that in our
world personal development recaps historical development
in another way too: from childhood into adulthood and then
on until death, a person's centre of psychic gravity tends to

rise from the belly up through the chest and neck and into the head, just as the Western world's centre of psychic gravity has been rising headward — skyward — over the last few thousand years, and especially since the Renaissance, and Gutenberg.

It's common knowledge that we have a physical centre of gravity, a point of balance in the body, and that it's situated in the groin or lower gut; I find it useful to think of our centres of psychic gravity as starting in the same place but then breaking away, for better *and* for worse, and embarking on a slow upward migration towards the rarefied, abstract spheres of the cerebrum. In the case of the individual, the centre of psychic gravity — the self, if you like, the soul — may rise upward until the person inhabits only a tiny portion of himself, herself, and seems somehow absent, like some bent, brittle miser who has removed to the attic room of his mansion and left the rest empty, sofas shrouded, tables ashen with dust. In the case of a society like ours, the collective psyche is forging upward, out of sight, like a space shuttle or Apollo — the soul of the community receding into ethers of abstraction.

I began to think and worry about where my own centre of psychic gravity was, and where it was getting to, a few years ago when I was suffering from neck problems ranging from painful kinks and spasms to mummifying seizures that would immobilize me for days. In flat mechanical terms the pain was the outcome of a sedentary life with many hours spent head-hunched over the page or the keyboard. But according to the magic realist conceit that soon occurred to me, my neck troubles were caused either by pressure as my own centre of psychic gravity bored upward through my neck into my head — a kind of birth, though sterile, and when I look back on what I was writing that year my intuitions are confirmed — or else by the psychic wedge I was unconsciously driving between body and head.

As a poet — or someone who wanted to call himself that, though his work was becoming increasingly abstract, less grounded, less sensuous — I was prepared to believe that even the most fanciful models and metaphors can embody deep psychological truths, so I took this lyrical diagnosis of mine in earnest. Still, it's only now that I can see the connection between the neck pains that summer, my sense that as a writer and a man I was beginning to ossify (like a body prematurely aged by the upward mobility of the soul into terminal abstraction), and my seemingly frivolous and pre-collegiate decision to join a local track club and start training again for one-mile races. And not only with the club, but on my own. Not only on the track but in the forests around Kingston, whenever I could get there, and by mountain bike on the roads, and by swimming, June to September, in the lakes and old quarries to the north.

My neck pain did not go away — it still hasn't — but the actual spasms grew rare, and then ceased. I felt fresher, clearer, less diffused, and though at the time I couldn't tell if my writing was starting to flow again in the same way, I think now, looking back, that it was. If the challenge every poet and fiction writer faces daily in this fact-obsessed, dream-hating "First World" is to find a way to jump-start the machinery of dreams, then the related, long-term challenge, for most of us, is to find a way to drive our centre of psychic gravity back out of the head into a more central place, where it can flourish in contact with both body and brain and serve as an integrating nexus between them.

The life of the mind, in its fullest, richest sense, *is* the life of the body; still, I sometimes crave, with a kind of animal nostalgia, a more purely physical life, and perhaps I would have chosen that life if this writing had not chosen me. Because I like the slow discipline that training imposes and then the sweet release and freedom of a full-out sprint, whether swimming in a lake or running on a golf course (barefoot is best). I love the way the concentration and exhilarating speed and the feel and sound of the wind drive out every petty, passing thought, so that "the earth," as William Saroyan put it, "is again now."

And when thought does return it's calmer, clearer, more grounded and concrete. There is that good cyclical easy fatigue at the end of the day and the sense that primary, terrestrial rhythms are never far from you — that intimate commerce with the elements is not just some atavistic or pseudomystical trope.

The best poetry and fiction, whether overtly concerned with sex or not, is erotic in the fullest sense of the word — in the rich sense that Lewis Hyde and Audre Lorde use the word. Eros is estranged from those who withdraw from their own bodies into the garret of the skull, but athletes know it as the partner in their dance. As poets do too. I think I might have liked to be a runner full-time; I think dabbling the way I now do helps me write better. As the great sprinter Eric Liddell is said to have asked the skull-tenants and calcified clergy of his parish who urged him to direct more of his time into conventionally pious works, "But why? God made me to work, but he also made me fast. And when I run, I feel His pleasure."

("*Training for the Millennium*" *appeared in the fifteenth anniversary issue of* Brick: A Literary Journal. *Writers were asked to consider what they might have been had they not become writers.*)

# 5

# The Age of Clowns

*At the German frontier, I stopped in the gabled platz of Braunau on the Inn and walked the few hundred yards to Hitler's birthplace. . . . The Hitler apartment has tactfully been turned into a children's library, and I could glimpse the side of Big Bird's head through the window amid stacks of neatly piled books and primary-colored building blocks. In the street stood a lump of stone to mark the site, piously dedicated to the victims of fascism, scrubbed free of furtive graffiti and the stains of hastily dropped bouquets.*
                                                     — Nicholas Fraser

I

THROUGHOUT THE 1980s a one-mile footrace was held each November down Princess Street in Kingston. The McDonald's Corporation — perhaps in hopes of softening up City Council, which had so far excluded its restaurants from the historical downtown core — had assumed sponsorship, and the race was called the McMile.

The year I entered the McMile — 1984 — the sponsors and organizers were trying to expand and popularize the event by adding a playful new dimension: runners were now encouraged to compete in costume, and laurels would be awarded not only to the fit and the swift but also to the frolicsome and preposterous.

I arrived at the starting line in nothing more preposterous than running shoes and sweats. Standing there among the yetis and the samurai, the Ronald McDonalds, the romping skeletons and self-propelled condoms, I felt as stiff and lost and stodgy as a neatly groomed Jehovah's Witness who knocks and is let in to some manic frat party. I hadn't heard about the costume element. I had come in earnest, as I went everywhere in those days. I was a student and an aspiring poet, at once dreamy and serious, always fervent about art and the mission of the artist and the new era that art might help forge. Shuffling up to the starting line with the colourful field and a few dozen serious runners — each stripped down, like me, to shorts and singlet and flashy shoes — I did not see that I and the other Spartans looked every bit as strange as the Giant Pandas and frogmen and mad scientists hemming us in. But I had trained conscientiously for this moment and, hard as it was to keep a straight face, I tried to stay focused. I meant to run my best time ever — my PB, as serious runners say. This feat seemed mortally important to me. I had not run seriously for a few years, but in 1984, buried alive in schoolwork and fearing that academic rhythms and habits of hyperanalysis were getting into my blood, I took it up again as a grounding discipline, a kind of visceral tonic or antivenin — so that, as with so many writers who take up a sport, sickness was my starting block.

I tensed on the starting line and waited for the gun. Behind the front rank of earnest Spartans, a festive, bantering horde with no intention of observing the usual pre-gun hush. Rambunctious laughter, a whiff of sweet liquor — a bottle being passed? — and the steady impersonal pressure from behind.

The starter had his pistol raised but he was holding back. Hoping for calm? Something caught my eye and I glanced to my right: a few runners away, a large chartreuse lizard, or crocodile, had pushed its way to the front and was crouched for the gun, puny forelegs eagerly flexed, squat thighs tensed and primed. The huge corrugated snout was aimed my way and the beady eyes seemed fixed on mine, as if issuing a challenge. For a moment I was transfixed. The gun cracked and the crowd lunged into motion, I was caught off-balance and went down amid thrashing elbows, knees, feet, and tails. Something barged into me and crashed over my back. The Hamburglar. I struggled to rise. By the time I got up, the lizard was well ahead and racing away with the leaders, its squat hind legs pumping like pistons, fat foam tail wagging back and forth as it dragged and bounced over the pavement.

I gave chase. The man in the lizard suit seemed a real runner — albeit one with a sense of humour — and he had a head start. Friends were awaiting me at the ribbon; the shameful prospect of finishing back of a waddling reptile spurred me on. I wanted to be that young hero in the Housman poem, "To an Athlete Dying Young," the one who wins the race for his town, and I wanted to pass and put out of sight that tail — that obscene fleering appendage whose every wag seemed a slap in the face. Saying to me: What the hell are you doing out here? What are you trying to prove? The time for this kind of thing — in your life, in the world's — is gone.

But the runner in the suit was not for real. Pulling even and passing him a hundred metres on, I shot him a smart, cocky glance. From inside the snout, a muffled, high-pitched wheezing. The beady eyes swivelling to meet mine. The little forelegs pumping frantically.

I did go on to run my PB but there were others faster.

2

IF THE ORWELLIAN DATE 1984 — which happened to be the year of that footrace — was touted by journalists and career catastrophists as a special one, the millennial year 2000 is sure to be pondered and augured even more thoroughly. Yet in the end 2000 is only a date, a number. For those unmoved by numerological symmetries and superstitions what matters about the date is how it happens to flag the final stage of an historical cycle, the stage we're living through now — the Age of Clowns.

In *The Decline of the West* Oswald Spengler argued that the basic biological pattern — of birth, flowering, and maturity followed by a slow decline into rigidity and death — can be applied to anything that exists in time: a human life, of course, but also the life of a solar system or a planet, a love affair, a career, a five-year sitcom or a Thousand-Year Reich, a revolution or a poker party.

Spengler applied his model primarily to civilizations, and especially the civilization of the West, but he never spoke of an "Age of Clowns"; he wasn't living in the heart of one. It seems to me — as the product and student of such an age — that the lives of civilizations and persons alike pass through a cycle involving an Unconscious Age (or "Age of Heroes," to use Spengler's term), an Age of Integration, an Age of Disintegration, and an Age of Clowns. In individual terms the roughly corresponding categories would be childhood/youth, maturity, old age, then senility and death. In historical terms the Bronze Age and the Dark Ages are Unconscious or "Heroic" times — the ones we glimpse in Homer and Herodotus, in the Old Testament, in *The Battle of Maldon* and *Beowulf.* If the Book of Genesis declares that "There were giants in the earth in those days," the other authors, each in a different manner, are saying the same thing. And though we only glimpse such epochs in a dauntingly mediated way, and we can't help sensing how the dusts of time and the will to nostalgia have blurred and elongated the inhabitants into giants roaming the Sinai or contesting "the plains of windy Troy," we still get the impression of a radically foreign sensibility, a deeply different people. Unconscious, or at least un*self*conscious, in a way we can hardly conceive. Not giants, but people of an inflated sense of honour, an aggressive ardency, almost unthinkable courage, and a marked lack of irony. This is an age where people live, like children or fervent youths, viscerally — a useful mode when it comes to romance, war, and the writing of unselfconscious bardic poems, but one which also dictates that people's lives are brutal, humourless, Spartan and autocratic. Intensely felt, but nasty and short.

The Age of Integration, in the Classical world, sees the flourishing of Periclean Athens and, later, of Augustan Rome. Now irony and a civilized sense of proportion have taken the blade-edge off the Unconscious Age and its savagery, but the irony is still fresh, humane, far from reaching the nihilistic, devitalizing pitch it will finally rise to. This is a time when — as Eliot claimed of a later Age of Integration, in Renaissance Europe — no "dissociation of sensibility" has set in, and people can still "think their feelings and feel their thought." This is a time when art flourishes, and not just for the benefit of an educated elite; Shelley's later boast that poets are "the unacknowledged legislators of the world" did not fully fit the situation in his time, and does not fit ours at all, but embodies a nostalgia for Classical and Renaissance Ages of Integration when poets were still socially important, when the aesthetic was not yet split off from the ethical, the poetic from the political.

An Age of Disintegration gradually sets in. The old borders of the empire buckle and contract. As the sense of communal cohesion and responsibility fails, the priest, the pharaoh, the senator, the president are guided more and more by a self-interest which hastens the process of decay. Still, for artists this is a fertile time. Even as their audience fragments and drifts away, the sense of impending apocalypse and the usefully disorienting pressures of life in limbo — between the old world of integration and the coming dark age — whet their efforts with political urgency and personal passion. But as things fall apart and the centre fails to hold, the Age of Disintegration shades imperceptibly into the cycle's terminal phase, the Age of Clowns, where citizens hide their confusion and pain behind comic masks and snarky punchlines, where the emperor fiddles as Rome burns, where jugglers and dwarves and trained bears dance for rich couples fornicating among the vomitoria as the Visigoths sweep down from the north.

The jesters themselves are a symptom, not a cause, and likeable in their own way, even noble, like those rodeo-clowns who distract the bull from the fallen bronco rider — but their sudden ubiquity and hellbent capering, hand in hand with the Grim Reaper, are signs that the bracing, vital irony of the Age of Integration has cancered into glibness and cynicism, anomie, a claustrophobic and sterile self-consciousness.

Now the culture can produce little important art. There are as many brave creative spirits as ever, but for them the freshness and spontaneity that good art requires, along with the artist's essential self-trust, are fraught commodities, while their faith in the ultimate relevance of art is lost. Or they turn from the very idea of ultimacy because it seems not merely authorial but authoritarian, imperialistic. But when artists stop trying to mean, art begins to wither. Heroic ages and their aftermaths produce largely unselfconscious and visceral works like the Norse sagas and the *Bhagavad Gita*; Ages of Integration give us writers of Classical confidence like the poets Sappho, Virgil, and Dante, and the dramatists Sophocles, Shakespeare, and Molière; Ages of Disintegration "hurt into poetry" anxious, rootless writers like T. S. Eliot, Gertrude Stein, W. H. Auden, and W. B. Yeats.* In the Age of Clowns it's far more difficult for writers to produce anything of deep value, partly because the culture refuses to value anything deeply, partly owing to the climate of futility and despair, and partly because some of the artists themselves are too busy winking at their own reflections, in the ceiling mirrors, during the orgy.

Until the Corporate Hordes and the Technogoths batter down the doors and usher in another dark age, or "unconscious civilization," to use John Ralston Saul's term.

For a more recent version of the pattern, or a subcycle within the larger pattern, consider the United States, its bloody and reverent Heroic Age running from settlement

---

* In Virgil's *Aeneid* it's fascinating to see a self-assured, self-consciously literary author, very much the product of an Age of Integration, emulating a voice from the Heroic Age — the voice of Homer, whoever he was. At any rate the highly visceral and unselfconscious sensibility of Homer's *Iliad* gives that poem an organic, dreamlike quality — as if, like Athena, it sprang fully formed from the head of a god — while Virgil's work feels wholly (and beautifully) artificial.

till the Revolution; its Age of Integration (given voice in Hawthorne, Thoreau, Emerson, Melville, Whitman, Wharton, Dickinson, and James) riding out the Civil War and lasting till after the First World War (which likewise ended the "Pax Britannica" and Britain's Age of Integration); its era of social and cultural disintegration gaining momentum through the years of the Great Depression, being interrupted by the briefly unifying Second World War, finding its centre, ground zero, with the birth of the bomb, and then forging on and culminating in the debacle in Vietnam. Stein, Fitzgerald, Faulkner, Nathanael West, Flannery O'Connor, and Thomas Pynchon are some major poets of the decline. Bring on the Clowns — like President Nixon, and Ronald Reagan, great emperor of the final phase, a B-actor with padded shoulders instead of padded, floppy shoes; *Bozo Meets Bonzo* the film he never made — and the cycle is fulfilled, though of course it isn't so kempt and symmetrical as I've made it sound, its latter phases especially being skewed by the many upheavals of our anomalous century.

If the aesthetic era known as "modernist" can be aligned with the Age of Disintegration, the postmodern era is coeval with the Age of Clowns. When pain without purpose has made the world retreat behind a leering mask and has set the word "love" in quotation marks. When self-consciousness becomes an end in itself, a dead-end, rather than a means to greater self-knowledge. When society's annual and essential self-parody, in time of Carnival, has become a year-round routine of smarmy and heartless street theatre or, on five hundred channels, a round-the-clock round-the-calendar festival of vacuity. When the artist's duty of discerning and expressing human meaning of one kind or another seems obsolete since the vast majority would rather read *People* for the latest update on the clownish Royals. When "virtual" realities crowd out visceral realities and the passionate context of nature and the body. When it becomes impossible to stay earnest and reverent about anything without looking like a dupe or a dangerous fanatic.

Clearly in the case of my one-mile race back in '84 — a few months after the L.A. Olympics had made a travesty of all Classical Olympic ideals — my collision with the mode of the carnivalesque was a healthy one, the lizard my comic doppelganger, reminding me to lighten up, to accept that the Unconscious, Heroic Age is long dead, that nostalgia is a limp and stultifying thing. Stultifying: from the Latin root for fool. "To be turned into a clown."

Five years after my run, while travelling in Turkey, I toyed with the idea of swimming the Hellespont and then writing an ironic essay on trying to follow in the footsteps, or in the wake, of Byron. My attitude towards the feat was not wholly ironic. I felt, in fact, that swimming the Hellespont would be a marvellous thing. I still do. But it was a long way across and I was told that anyone risking it would lose layers of skin to the pollution and then die of cancer, or be keelhauled by a Crimean oil tanker or hooked down by the periscope of a nuclear sub.

Besides, like everything else, it's been done.

I know there's no way back to some fresher Age of Integration, and as a child of a different time I could not feel at home there anyway; I know I would find its confidence haughty, its certainties and unities coercive, constraining, its hierarchies oppressive and unfair. But is it futile to dream of a new and fully humane Age of Integration? Is it possible to arrive there without first passing through a new Unconscious Age ruled over by Technogoths, Fundamentalists, feudal Multinationals, or whatever rough beast comes after them? Spengler's view of historical cycles was strictly deterministic and left little or no leeway for rejuvenating intervention — and artists, after all, are no longer legislators of any kind. The repeated upwelling this century of romantic nostalgia for a Heroic Age of Blood and Soil — most notably in fascist Italy, Germany, Japan, and in Stalinist Russia — along with the recent rise of militant fundamentalism all over the world, does suggest a growing resistance to modern life and to its sensibility, its complexities, its barren abstractions, its clinical self-consciousness. This hankering for creeds and heroes to spring us from the jail of over-consciousness may be a harbinger of the new cycle, a sign that the only road to another Age of Integration must pass through the shadow of the apocalypse and over the scorched earth of another Dark, Unconscious Age.

Perhaps the best that individual artists can do is to try to foster Ages of Integration in their own hearts. An integrated writer may not have the power to overthrow the centralized rule of the cynical and the grasping, but the power to move a few thousand people deeply is something, is much; in a world so fragmented, any gesture that radically connects mind to mind and heart to heart is hugely significant. And surely the first step for any writer who dreams of reaching the cells and cadres of the fed-up and the disaffected is to shun capitulation to the Disneyesque spirit of the age, to Casper, the friendly Zeitgeist; to refuse to fiddle around in cyberspace while the ghettoes burn; to remain a believer, unafraid of the unfashionably serious engagement with human joy and sorrow that still yields meaning and still seeds in readers the socially vital habit of empathy; to resist not only the virtual realities and cyberabstractions of post-modernity but also the atavistic impulse to heroic vitalism, that fascist denial of the modern world that seduced and so often stultified Eliot, Pound, D. H. Lawrence, and others.

To find a point of passionate integration between droll postmodern self-awareness and a hankering for the primal ooze.

In the Book of Revelations John of Patmos lays out a febrile and surrealistic dreamscape of apocalyptic figments and portents that pulse with a sublime, uncanny grandeur; pushed along by a coked-up global capitalism, the Age of Clowns sprints on towards its own farcical apocalypse — though to the homeless relics tapping tambourines for quarters along the main street as the McMile surges past, the farce has no audible laugh-track. They shelter in boarded doorways, alleyways, so many of the downtown stores closing now as the centrifuge of the cycle's end hurls people out towards the malls and particle-board catacombs of the suburbs. True enough, the centre cannot hold. Meanwhile the parade scythes on down the main street of the century in a particoloured danse macabre and I stumble on against the wind with the other believers — all of us chilled, short of breath, and ridiculous — and the clowns close in behind.

# 6

# Apollo VI and the Flight from Emotion

*Since the days of the caves man has glorified and deified himself, and has brought about human catastrophe by his monstrous vanity. Art has collaborated in his false development. . . . The conception of art that has upheld the vanity of man is sickening. . . .*

— Hans Arp

THE RAPIDLY GROWING ABSTRACTION of electronic, post-industrial society goes on eroding the audience for all the arts while breeding conditions which make them more necessary than ever. Necessary because of the essential and redemptive concreteness of, for example, good poetry, fiction, and nonfiction. Which fewer and fewer read. This paradox — art's growing estrangement from a more and more needy public — lies close to the heart of the diseased body of the "developed" West and the diseased bodies of its citizens.

Strange to speak of diseased bodies, even in the age of HIV, when life expectancies in the "First World" are longer than ever. But the term is more than metaphorical. It signifies an affliction that's real enough, yet difficult to measure and assess: the spiritual-physical malaise that sets in when the human animal dislocates itself from the ground of its own body and of the earth around it.

"Human separatism" is the name I use for the notion that humankind is fundamentally separate from, and superior to, the rest of creation. This attitude finds one of its first and best-known expressions in the Book of Genesis, where humanity is granted dominion over the earth and all other living things. At best, this edict has helped lend a sense of dignity and distinction to human life, relieving some of the staple anxieties that have plagued us "since the days of the caves"; at worst it's been a mandate for catastrophe, having granted us ontological *carte blanche*, a sort of cosmic credit card whose indiscriminate use has grown especially dire now that we have the means to destroy life altogether.

"Mental separatism" is a natural offshoot of human separatism and involves the splintering off, in individuals, of the rational faculty from the intuitive and physical side of being. If ontogeny recapitulates phylogeny, as the biologists say, then the rapid evolution of mental separatism over the last few centuries is likewise a recapitulation of the way human separatism has grown over the last few millennia. Since the days of the caves almost all human development has involved a movement towards mind and its virtual realities, and away from the concrete, visceral reality that still forms the ground of our being — and the ground we live on, walk on, and finally return to. It's a process that might be said symbolically to start in Eden, with human interest in the Tree of Knowledge, which led Adam and Eve's eyes up through the boughs towards the heavens and away from the ground — towards reason and away from the body. Which they were suddenly ashamed of. Towards a remote, celestial god, away from the earth-goddess-worship of older societies.

The mental separatism which Plato helped father came back into its own with the Renaissance, picked up steam in the Industrial Revolution, and in our century has set in motion an exponential arc of further abstraction which now threatens all life — if not to destroy it altogether, then surely to leach all the poetry and joy from its veins.

*The mind is ashamed of the blood*, wrote D. H. Lawrence; and more than ever in this world that we've retooled, plugged in and booted up, the blood is destroyed by the mind.

> *Variety and quality are . . . disappearing . . . throughout all of the arts and society.* Rambo v *and chickens pumped full of hormones and antibiotics are closely related to Waldenbooks and [the creative writing workshop industry]. They are symptoms of the same disease . . . resulting from profit's disconnectedness from real production.*
>
> — August Kleinzahler

The process of abstraction from what is radically, organically real — this inexorable triumph of the artificial — continues apace in every area of life. Consider money, its origins in barter: a farmer takes five of your clay pots and, after some affable haggling, hands over three of his chickens. This concrete system of exchange undergoes its first abstract inflection some time later when the powers-that-be introduce coins of gold and silver to stand for the pots and chickens. Then for convenience, a few centuries after that, paper bills and tokens of brass or tin are introduced, all of them representing real gold secured in the coffers of the kingdom or, later still, in the vaults of Fort Knox. Then —

despite opposition — the gold standard is abandoned and the "tokens" are no longer tokens at all but "real" currency, as are the bills. Finally at an arts and crafts show in a tony urban shop, this process of abstraction is consummated when a speculator buys up all your handmade pots by flashing an essentially worthless shard of plastic.

Labour. In much of the world less and less of it is manual — physical — as our working lives grow increasingly mechanized, and now computerized. Again, a movement away from the body and into the mind (the computer being a further extension, and abstraction, of mind). Clearly this process has been a real advance and a blessing in many ways, but in practice a mixed one.

Food. The staples that were once hunted down, killed, stripped and cleaned and cooked over open fires, or later grown and harvested and readied by the hearth, are now canned or freeze-dried and pulled ready-to-eat from the computerized microwave. So that the bison our distant forebears ochred onto cave walls have been domesticated and disembodied into boneless, tasteless heat-and-serve nuggets that never embarrass diners by declaring their origins. The mind *is* ashamed of the blood. Or, as the scholar in Leonard Cohen's *Beautiful Losers* protests, "This isn't chicken, this is a chicken." (True enough, these days we're rarely gored while tracking down a meal, but much of the food we eat — like Kleinzahler's nuggets "pumped full of hormones," a foodstuff Brian Fawcett dubs "universal chicken" — may well get us in the end.)

As for the malls where such awful, degrading, denatured food is sold, they're likewise an abstraction. They're designed to insulate shoppers so comfortingly, so completely from the natural world that they forget all their old human insecurities and buy beyond credit with no thought of tomorrow or the health of a planet already congested with "goods" and garbage. Malls create an illusion of safety, of inexhaustible *plenty*.

From malls to the moon: in the celestial canons of astronomy and cosmology you can trace a parallel arc of abstraction from the simple, concrete Ptolemaic universe, where Earth sat smugly at the centre of things, through a Copernican universe centred on the sun, to a vast, entropic model where the sun is demoted to the substatus of a minor star in a local galaxy in a huge cosmos without centre — a vision of such daunting abstraction that only a handful of people are able or willing to comprehend it fully.

Ontologically, a move up and out of the caves, where what was real was the visible, tangible body, to Democritus' model of simple atoms, to the ether and electric fields of the nineteenth century, to the cyberspace and subatomic physics of today.

Sociopolitically an advance from the primitive pecking orders of the jungle and the cave to a kind of democratic socialism (in some countries) founded on abstract principles instead of primal, unmediated instincts and desires.

Again, many of these changes have been blessings, but the blessings have been deeply mixed. And indirectly they continue to spread the diseases and civilized discontents that Freud first delved into a century back. But while more and more people, hoping to heal and reintegrate themselves, are resorting to therapy or pharmaceuticals or the simplistic best-sellers of self-help gurus, few seek out the kind of music and painting and poetry and cinema that could help them as much, or more. And help the world besides, in some small way, since problems like tribalism, racism, and misogyny, which dualistic human separatist thinking advance and aggravate, won't be eased unless human separatism is

reassessed, and the world will not be "greened" again over-
night by people who are still self-divided mental separatists
— strangers to the "green fuse" in themselves. Ecological
issues are sexy these days and the bandwagon is rolling and
crowded, but fundamental change can only occur if a spiritual shift gives rise to a new attitude towards the body and
the earth.

Diseased, both of them.

And though the audience for all the arts continues to
atrophy, I go on believing art can help. (Not that art is *for*
that primarily — art isn't primarily for anything — but that's
what it does when it's good. Good art is a reconciler of
irreconcilable differences, a go-between bringing reason and
the senses back into the same room, the same heart —
bringing us back to ourselves and the things of this world
we'd grown to think ourselves separate from.)


> *The word was born in the blood.*
> — Pablo Neruda


In these disembodied times, while audiences go on shrink-
ing, the hunger for art continues to grow. More than ever
people need to reconnect with what's real and lasting —
inside themselves and outside in the world — and the arts,
because of their sensual concreteness, are uniquely equipped
to help. Dance is probably the most basic of all the arts, the
most physical and dynamic — but although the ground of
being is in the body, humans are also by nature rational and
verbal, and so the literary arts, because they're best furnished
to express, reflect, and engage the sum of our physical and
mental being, have a unique role to play in any mind-body
*rapprochement.*

All the same, a partisan of dance or music could argue that language itself is an abstraction and once written down exists at yet another remove from the world it purports to describe; and in fact, the written, printed word has played a central role in the evolution of mental separatism. More than that, this mind-body schism that has been widening since the Renaissance has affected the literary arts themselves and may have rendered them incapable of reconnecting us to anything. T. S. Eliot, in his famous essay on the Metaphysical poets, lamented the "dissociation of sensibility" marked by the alleged failure of English-speaking poets since Shakespeare's time to write work that was both visceral and thoughtful. Eliot argued that poets like John Donne were more whole both as writers and as people: neither dryly, coyly cerebral like the elegant salon wits of a century later, nor breast-beatingly anti-intellectual like some writers of the Romantic reaction in the century after that. Nowadays, too, it's common to characterize writers as either "intellectual," "formal," and "conservative," or else "passionate" and "romantic" and "physical" — or, to use Nietszche's dichotomy, as Apollonian or Dionysian. Yet the Metaphysicals, according to Eliot, were capable not only of feeling and of thinking but of "feeling their thought."

Eliot's notion is nostalgic and simplistic yet at the same time wonderfully fertile, relevant; clearly the kind of literary art best able to narrow the "dissociation of sensibility" still widening in our own time is art both passionate and intelligent. What else? Cool or coyly intellectual work can only contribute to the near-terminal process accelerating around us. A poem packed full of theory, but dead to the world of the senses, is a kind of capitulation, a collaboration with the enemies of the heart. Likewise the icy detached neoformalism currently in vogue with many British and American academic poets, like the worst examples of pat, precious, self-indulgent postmodernism, exemplify what John Metcalf has called "a flight from emotion" — which is to say a further flight from the body, from the ground of our being, from the organic and the authentic. From the earth.

"Flight." Metcalf can hardly be using the word, with all the implications our century has layered on to it, by accident. I think by using it he aligns formalist or postmodern intellectualism with the heartless, clinical complexity of the machine, the jetliner, the space shuttle, the Apollo.

In the next century it will be the near-impossible task of writers and other artists to bring at least a few people back down to earth.

Yet the very fact of literature's increasing institutionalization (another good example of abstraction) will continue to work against such groundings. Of course literature does need to be in the universities, and writers should be visiting more grade schools and high schools and libraries as well, but if the time comes — as Dana Gioia has predicted — when the university is the lone and last preserve of the poet, then literature really will have been rendered academic. In a more and more fractured and dis-integrated society, this academic quarantine, this progressive institutionalization could effectively demote the poet to the rank of court juggler or licensed fool.

> *Intellectual creation also springs from the physical.*
> — Rainer Maria Rilke

The literary arts will never have a large audience. Perhaps they never did. But they continue to play a living role in this postmodern world because they act as a counterpoise, however inadequate, to the growing bulk of meaningless information and superfluous, disposable consumer goods and high-tech gadgetry and other synthetic paraphernalia. Of course there are other, more popular alternatives, like fundamentalist religion with its consolingly authoritarian, atavistic certainties — but clearly such things can only add to the intolerance and spiritual fission of our time. On the other hand literature is uniquely armed to introduce each new generation of readers to the habit of empathy — of learning to see things through another's eyes and to feel with another's body and heart. Film has an instantaneous power that books can't match, and at its best it makes us see in startling new ways, but only literature can offer the kind of nuanced, qualified, many-dimensioned psychological insights that let us feel things, however briefly, with a stranger's heart.

Fresh poetic images that in some small way change forever the focus and range of the eye; how the inviting openness or alarming finality of a novel's conclusion reawakens readers to the course of their own lives, the possibilities of a life. How the rhythm and music of a poem rewaken sedentary readers to the half-forgotten metres of their own pulses, while certain lines of poetry elicit a primitive, physical response — cause shivering, tears, cause hairs to hackle on the forearm. Re-embody us. Reconnect us to real life.

In the context of our techno-obsessive, disembodied times this effect is highly subversive — even, or especially, if the work that induces it seems apolitical. Or call the effect redemptive, as I did at the beginning of this essay, or call it moral as George Woodcock does; the implications are the same. In a state that functions largely by keeping its citizens sedated with an endless supply of tawdry toys and disposable "goods," big-budget schlock and other forms of virtual reality, the effect of dynamic writing is to rehumanize readers, to revive them to the real goods inside and around themselves. Our most important poets are the ones who aren't afraid to sing — to draw their words and rhythms from that profound, unfashionable source our civilization has spent so many centuries trying to wall off. You know the one I mean — the place genuine laughter erupts from when something is explosively funny, the thing that ambushes you with wrenching sobs at the funeral of an old friend.

Needless to say there are many ways to sing — many keys, many pitches. The ironic and restrained but authentic emotion of Don Coles's love poems or of Emily Dickinson's austere, brief epitaphs or of bp Nichol's quiet elegies can form song as surely as G. M. Hopkins or Gwendolyn Mac-Ewen or Michael Ondaatje with their more lavish and vatic propensities. But all are relevant, all are song, all act to bridge the widening gap between the reader's heart and mind.

"Writing from the body" is how some postmodern theorists describe visceral, kinetic work, and though their writings on the theme are often needlessly — and self-deconstructively — abstract and inaccessible, the phrase itself is a good one. As Michael Holmes argues, we need more fiction writers with the courage to reject the orthodoxy of the day, which holds that a chilly, carefully filtered intellectual detachment from character and situation is the mature, and modern, way to write.

*Exuberance is Beauty.*
— Blake

In the beginning was the Word, begins the New Testament, and in essence that phrase is a skewed echo — abstracted by several millennia and the intervening growth of knowledge and literacy — of the Old Testament assertion that God gave man dominion over all things. Because, obeying the Word of God, Adam set names to all living things and so established the primacy of Word — *logos*, reason — over Body (symbolized by the animals he named). But V. S. Naipaul points out that in parts of Africa the equivalent phrase runs "in the beginning was the Drum" — and if that means, as it must, that in the beginning was the first faint pulse in the womb, the beating heart, the secret metres of the body and its cells, then the African phrase expresses an older, earthier, more elemental truth. Not better or more true, but surely less abstracted. Closer to the Africa of our origins, where our bodies still dwell.

These words and thoughts are part of a search for balance, passionate balance at the heart's true centre, not a plea for some kneejerk, neoromantic reaction against postmodernity. Whatever drumbeating in woodlots may be doing for novices in the Men's Movement, it's not a panacea for the world's ills. Naturally we can't all go back to living in straw huts and bartering chickens for clay pots and being stirred — often as far as violence — by the village bard's chanting or the blood and soil rhetoric of demagogues; all the same, sensuous, dynamic, embodied writing does have a role to play in effecting a partial reconciliation between the modern mind and the timeless body — our own, and the earth's — from which it has been abstracted.

The body, in the words of Wallace Stevens, is the great poem.

# 7

# The Electrocution of the World

EVOLUTION — personal, spiritual, and cultural, if not biological — involves the interplay of two conflicting impulses,
on the one hand the will to explore and struggle and change,
and on the other the will to conserve energy and seek a state
of order, security, and rest. New forms or movements dominated by either impulse may seem evolutionary, but not all
of them are. Think of two people in the grips of so-called
midlife crises who leave their families — the first because his
or her marriage and home life really do seem unsalvably
damaged and the flowing and growth of love in the marriage
have ceased, a kind of spiritual gangrene setting in; the
second because the relationship has reached that crucial
point where a focused mutual effort is needed to push things
upward to a new level, and instead the choice is made to
leave, to light out and ride the bumpy but uncomplicated
carnival-coaster of honeymoon love through a series of summer fair relationships.

Dramatic choice — in fact change of any kind — can seem
to have the weight of evolutionary necessity behind it, yet
often the implications are devolutionary. I'll admit I'm distorting things here for the sake of argument, oversimplifying

as one always does when using people as exemplary types; but if for a second we turn from the warping funhouse mirror, suspend disbelief and gaze into the future, we're apt to find the first person evolving through honest struggle into a fiercened and disabused maturity while the second one — the one whose choices were dominated by a fear of effort and of suffering change — remains stalled, baffled, narcissistic, and narrow.

So in the face of any evolving form it's worth considering which of the two impulses dominates — the dynamic and aspiring, or the static and conservative. A changing life or form dominated by the first will likely survive and keep on evolving; a changing life or form driven by the second is apt to stagnate, petrify, and perish.

Today's changing literary forms can be considered in the same light.

Literary form is always evolving in more than one direction at once, but most of the changes we've seen over the last century have stemmed, directly or indirectly, from technology's steady advance. If aesthetic modernism was a belated response to the urbanization, industrialization, and secularization of the world, postmodernism is likely a response to and a function of more advanced electronic technologies like television and the computer, the relativizing effects of twentieth-century physics and philosophy, and the "information explosion" — a conflux of phenomena which, though not without redeeming features, forms the main current in a surging global process I call "the electrocution of the world." And if modernism and early postmodernism entailed an adaptation of literature to a changed world, some more recent isms seem to me a kind of capitulation, a kind of giving over of literature to the most oppressive, alienating, and injurious elements of high-tech culture.

Most of the literary forms evolving today are conceptual and artificial rather than visceral and organic, and most of them, in sync with the caffeinated tempo of our time, are evolving and mutating too fast to really track. During the six years I spent reading manuscripts for *Quarry Magazine* I saw several literary fashions rise and fall and various issues vise-grip the public imagination then slacken their hold, but underlying these theme-oriented trends was a general "evolution" towards sectional fragmentation, increasing brevity, increasing simplicity and sameness of vocabulary, punctuation, and syntax, and a growing absence of concrete sensuous detail — a drift into the dry and lifeless spheres of the abstract.

The abstraction and deracination of society that stirred up Blake, Marx, Sartre, Pound, and more recent writers like Edward Abbey, Joseph Beuys, and Allucquere Roseanne Stone, continues to develop, and in this electronic age, where everything changes apace, their rate of growth is exponential. The evolution of societal abstraction has special implications for the literary arts because writing — unlike painting, or sculpture, or music — must avoid abstraction if it is to affect readers physically and thus "stay read."* But how can writers raised in such an abstract milieu not be affected? How can they maintain contact with the earth's elemental energies and the kindred energies of the human unconscious when the brainmade world around them, abuzz with jarring, jamming signals and short-circuiting

---

* I take this wonderful phrase of Merilyn Simonds's as meaning "to continue to resonate in the life and survive in the memory of the individual reader" — though in the broader political sense "staying read" is as much a function of academic and curricular prejudice as it is of merit.

electronic distractions, automatically hypes and underwrites the artificial?

If one of the primary aims of every artist is to communicate with people and to move them, arouse them, reopen dozing eyes not for the quick fix of a few moments but in a lasting way, then surely formal evolution that fails to produce work with staying power is, from an aesthetic standpoint, not evolution but devolution. But what does stay read? Recently in the *New Yorker* Janet Malcolm, writing about the American artist David Salle, considered the tendency of some postmodern art to impress powerfully at first but then to "sour" and fade in the memory. I have the feeling that many readers have had that same fade-to-black experience with recent paintings, and books — an experience that until recently I tended to associate with the better grade of Hollywood film. But if films like *Schindler's List* will pale with time because they're formulaic, superficial, and manipulative, much postmodern work — especially the kind I think of as televisual — will fade out for another reason. As anyone who pursues a sport over a long period knows, there is such a thing as muscular memory, and over time it's more precisely retentive than the brain, on its own, can be. Facts eventually fade in the brain but the body's memory endures. So that a story or poem written with the whole being, and in sensuous terms, is experienced viscerally by a reader and better remembered, for longer.

Arguing that the body always remembers is not to imply that the brain is mystically uninvolved in the writing of poetry and fiction; ideally the brain and body form an integrated, organic whole and work together, so that, in T. S. Eliot's nostalgic formulation, we think our feelings and feel our thought. But in a world where brain and body are so rigidly sequestered it takes a huge effort of will and concentration to reconcile one's halves in the act of writing and so produce work that might "stay read." It takes a stubborn and patient writer and one determined to avoid all shortcuts — the kind of technological or institutional quick fixes our culture is always trying to sell.

Word processors do offer a writer certain shortcuts, but those aren't the kind I mean. A serious writer can work just as well with a computer as with a typewriter, and maybe better, provided the machine is viewed as an editorial tool and not as a crutch or a fetish. (And if it's true that cathode-ray monitors induce dreamy alpha-wave activity in the brains of those sitting in front of them, it might be interesting for poets, especially, to work on them, at least for a first draft — though personally I still prefer to start out longhand. Hands on.)

No, the problem with electronic media in terms of writers and their evolving forms is that the media have pushed to the forefront and now lead the Western world's march into terminal abstraction, and the effect of this process is, predictably, to make writers more abstract, more detached from the sensual sources of imaginative power, more mediated — more remote and controlled. For forty years now, and despite its name, television has been eroding our capacity for vision by framing an image of the world that's largely formulaic, stereotyped, flat, and blandly secular. Visual clichés blur the eye just as aural clichés dull the ear — and, as Neil Postman has remarked, watching TV is the one human activity at which it's impossible to get any better. Meanwhile scene-bite video offers an even more fleeting focus on the world, or what little we glance of it, as it infects the eye with a violently accelerated and hostile impatience.

Most of the literary forms evolving today signal a kind of mindless capitulation to this addictive and antihuman trend, an opportunistic pimping to ever shorter attention spans. Most of the new forms symptomize our growing blindness to the world.

If electrocution kills an organism by short-circuiting the heart, the electrocution of the world is a similar process whereby the hearts of people en masse are short-circuited and rendered dysfunctional. Or worse. Writers do have to be searching for new forms, new ways of seeing and saying, and postmodernism has given us some good ones, but now that it's calcifying into an orthodoxy its emphasis on theory and self-consciousness and skeptical dissection should be regarded with — what? What else? Skepticism. Good artists tend to give the world what it doesn't have enough of instead of things it has too much of already, and besides, as Erin Mouré has said, evolution occurs "on the margins of organization" — and in the academy postmodernism is now the mainstream.

No evolution there. In art as in life the path of least resistance always leads indirectly but finally to the backwater, the boneyard, the attic chest. Yet how else to proceed? Digging deeper into the heart and the imagination involves a labour both spiritual and physical — two kinds of work we're out of shape for in this terminally secular, and sedentary, world. And the attraction of the evolving, electronically influenced forms is among other things their *ease*.

To return to that dichotomy of struggle and ease, of dynamism and stasis, I'd argue that many of the newer forms — like "language-centred" poetry and the critical theory that fuels it, or the more academic or televisual forms of postmodern fiction — are attractive to writers partly because they're easier to write. I've written samples myself, so I feel I know. In fact on first encountering the Cooveresque story-in-short-televisual-sections I was instantly attracted — and not because I saw in the form a reflection of my generation's reality but, I think, because of a young writer's perfectly natural desire for shortcuts.

The literary forms "evolving" under the influence of the high-tech media are primarily cerebral and conceptual in nature. By demoting the unpredictable heart from the creative process and buckling Brain and Will into the pilot's seats, they allow writers to feel more in control of their material than ever before. A hard offer to turn down. Especially in a time so willful as ours, so obsessed with control. Likewise the quickness, glibness, and channel-surfing shifts typical of these forms free a writer from the ornery obligation to look long and hard at things, at characters, at scenes, to stare stubbornly and patiently until life surges into vital focus — to stare the way Flannery O'Connor insisted all writers should stare, since "there is nothing that does not require [your] vision." In turn this freedom from the artist's duty to maintain deep and sustained focus — this freedom from the need for passionate vision and inspiration — allows a writer to churn stuff out, anytime, anywhere: a real advantage in a world so obsessed with product and in institutions where one's survival really may depend on regular publication. Finally many of the new forms come furnished with a justifying and exculpating theoretical framework that comforts a writer with a sense of membership and community while excusing or whiting-out any weakness in the writing: *my politics are too important for any pettifogging aesthetic complaints.* The inclusive politics in question may be valid and humane, but I'm wary of how frameworks and isms of any kind make it lethally easier to write, easier to rationalize or ignore one's shortfalls and blind spots instead of confronting them. So the attraction here is inherently static and conservative — not revolutionary, not even evolutionary — like the choice of that man or woman who abandons long-term challenge for the short slick sectional stories of more facile relationships.

Theoretical forms of writing are a kind of game, like Tetris, a kind of virtual reality; as I've urged, they allow a writer to create using only the brain — a process far less demanding than submitting to real, full-body inspiration and the torments (and special pleasures) of honest re-vision. It's like choosing to analyze the marathon, in uncrackable jargon, after watching one on TV — instead of running one first and then struggling to describe it.

In my last years as an editor I saw more and more stories and poems that amounted to a kind of literary MTV — they were sleek and shifting, quick and gadgety. I could have filled the pages I was editing with competent examples, by truly talented writers, of this "tough, urban" writing, this so-called sudden fiction. Suddenly read, suddenly forgotten, but that hardly matters, as readers weaned on TV and videos we'll think we're getting the real thing and maybe if we went and tried to read, say, Alice Munro or Keath Fraser, we'd have real trouble, would grow impatient for the payoff, the climax, the wrap-up and credits, and on to the next channel.

Click.

The predicament of my generation of readers can be compared to that of the trapped tenants of Plato's cave — the ones who mistook their own shadows on the wall for reality. If all we see are flickering shadows on a screen, or on a page, then we'll draw from them what sustenance and comfort we can, as we must; we'll be aware that something is missing in our lives but unable to pinpoint the deficiency and in the meantime we'll make a big noise praising the more interesting shadows and disprizing the more feeble. But most of what we see will be feeble, since shadows are a bloodless fax of the real world just as glib gadgety writing is a mere ghost of that art which engages the world in a concrete and passionate way (and not always in a conventionally "realistic" or linear manner, either).

One solution — or mode of resistance — is to fight our way back down towards the source, the undomesticated deep levels of being not yet short-circuited in the world's electrocution. But how? Our now-customary reliance on high-tech paraphernalia to solve problems has made us unaccustomed to searching within ourselves, in silence — patiently — the way someone like poet and monk Tim Lilburn seems willing to do. Though perhaps even if we did break through to the fountainhead we would find the waters there more than a little tainted by seepage from the levels above?

No. I don't think so. I think there's still a level untainted, untouched.

Still, the difficulty in reaching that source in a disembodied age may help explain the importance of the "borrowings" or outright stealings in "intertextual" or "collaborative" modern and postmodern art. Though Western artists like Paul Simon have forged some remarkable music through their collaborations and hybridizations, the manifestly growing impulse of Western artists to borrow from Africa and Asia is not only a sign of admiration but of enervation — clear evidence of the psychic depletion and spiritual famine we've brought on ourselves over the last few centuries (over which time, not incidentally, physical famine has become a far graver reality in colonized Africa and Asia). The problem is not with cross-influence and collaboration per se — they always have been a key part of the creative process — but that the temporarily enriching effects of this borrowing, this "shot in the arm," may help keep us blind to the accruing soullessness of our post-industrial world. More and more our own wellsprings are polluted or paved over; where will we dig for sustenance once Asia is paved over too?

One form T. S. Eliot popularized and which enjoys even greater popularity today is the collage — the poem that consists essentially of pieces taken from other, usually older poems, or sometimes from popular media. As *The Waste Land* shows, the result can be compelling and mysterious, but the trend itself is disturbing — a symptom of depletion and degeneracy, as Eliot recognized himself. As years pass and I read more widely I discover piece by piece that all the soaring high points of *The Waste Land* derive from somewhere else — usually the earnest, ingenuous heartcries of less sophisticated but more authentic, less mediated souls (like Sappho, from whom, I recently discovered, Eliot filched much of the beautiful "hyacinth girl" scene at the end of *The Waste Land*'s first section). Eliot's technique did raise eyebrows at the time, but in our day "intertextuality" has become a given — and to many critics the very measure of a work's validity. Yet while a poem or novel can only be enriched by its author's passionate dialogue with other writers, living or dead, in the work of an authentic artist most of the high points, soaring or not, are original, not just airlifted in from some cavernous mental hangar when inspiration drags.

Some would say that in our age the kind of "originality" I'm talking about is unthinkable because of the information explosion, because we live in a polyphonic global village, because the babbling unremittant currents of the mass media are in our homes and our hearts and inescapable. So while Emily Dickinson could live and write alone with only her Bible, her hymnbook, and her starkly idiosyncratic vision, we are driven into constant collaboration with others whether we want it or not. Well, maybe. But even if it's true that some intertextuality is natural and nourishing, that doesn't preclude freshness of vision save for those who use the theory of the intertext as an excuse not to struggle after their own means, their own voices. And if what it takes to mine down to the source and start speaking eccentrically is to retreat into the hills, like Tim Lilburn, and dig a pit in the ground and climb down and sit in darkness and wait, listening — staring — can a writer afford not to try?

Not necessarily that, of course, but something.

Intertext, interface, Internet, interactive. So much easier to be inter than to be inside. Seems the electronic knocking of the phone or the fax always comes just in time to save us from a painful collision with ourselves. Our souls. That Person from Porlock always knocking, the vital job forever left undone.

Don't get me wrong, "interactivity" is good as far as it goes, but eccentric and uncompromising individuality has always been at the root of lasting art and remains the one force to hold off the homogenizing, levelling pressures of the online age. An age of big institutions and governments. An age where the human body with all its anarchic, un-governable sense energies is being disappeared, the visceral replaced by the virtual, the corpus subsumed by the Cor-poration. Devoured. So maybe the leggy tangle of recent erotic fiction contests and erotic anthologies, good though some of them are, is part of an anxious, eleventh-hour grop-ing back towards Eros, the body, the earth — not unlike Wild Man Weekends and bongo drumming in the woods. Like those things the new erotica seems part of a reaction against the theorization of the world, the ongoing electro-cution, the evisceration of everything.

Of course there are good theory-driven and techno-driven

writers (and the two types are flip sides of the same page), but it's not the theory or gadgetry that makes them interesting, it's how their love of the world somehow seeps into the work through the tight mesh of theory, or through the wires of the machine.

I'm not against theory as such, I'm against a mindset that puts theory before love.

I believe the literary forms being evolved under the influence of the electronic media are part of an evolutionary dead-end: like Eohippus and the Neanderthal, they're doomed. But while we can only guess as to why those other defunct life forms failed to thrive, it's possible in the case of some postmodern or televisual forms to lay a wager: all ideological excuses and special pleading aside, most of the forms signal a pact with abstraction and a retreat from emotion and vivifying struggle — not unlike the person leaving his or her family for the rollercoaster ride that finally ends in an empty fairground among shadows and blowing newspaper and tramped cans and rusting machinery. And that other one, who leaves because she has to, and hurts for it, and maybe walks east like the man in Rilke's poem in search of the true life of the spirit and the heart "that his father forgot" — that writer or any writer who opts to struggle with what does not change will surely keep on edging forward. It's not what our world calls progress, as we go on entangling ourselves in the executioner's wires and nodes, but it might well be evolution of a kind.

# 8

# In the Suburbs of the Heart

In his introduction to Artie Gold's poetry collection *The Beautiful Chemical Waltz* George Bowering writes

> all the while most of the wide-scattered Canadian poets have never entertained the notion of asking the muses for anything. They think they can "express themselves" in tidy anecdotes about spouses in bed or toddlers in the autumn leaves.

And, in large numbers, they do. We do. After all, our society was founded by people who named the thoroughfares of our towns and cities Victoria Street, King Street, Clergy Street, Barracks Street, while in Québec, say, or in Mexico, even now you can veer off Church or King onto an Avenue of the Angels or the Martyrs or the Saints or the clouds. The muses, almost . . . But while Bowering may seem to be setting up a false polarity between "self-expression" and a more sublime, aspiring kind of work, or between the banal world of the domestic and the rarefied ethers of the "muse," he would no doubt be the first to admit there's no reason the muse shouldn't preside over poems about "toddlers in autumn leaves" or inhabit and eternalize a short story set, for example, by the kitchen sink. Bowering's complaint seems to be that the muse simply isn't invoked or involved; that most Canadian poetry has lacked the magical catalyst that can transfigure a domestic scene into something timeless; that many writers simply don't think of calling the muses down — or, to put it another, much riskier way, of calling things up from the dim, dream-webbed cellars and crawl spaces of the soul.

Riskier, yes, because "soul" is a word and a concept that never has been a staple of Canada's literary lexicon. But then Bowering's complaint about what I would call the suburban, secular, journalistic, and above all sensible quality of too much of our writing is retrospective; what can be said about new Canadian writing? Is it different in any way? I'm a fan of Canadian writing and have been from the time I was eighteen — reading Earle Birney's "David" during a climb in the Rockies — but as an insatiable reader and a former editor who dealt with over a thousand manuscripts a year from writers both new and established, I've come to share some of Bowering's complaints.

Like most Canadian children I was subtly drilled and slowly driven to become "nice" — dull and decent, unobtrusive, sober, compliant and blandly cooperative, robotically courteous, careful — and though attributes like decency and politeness are obviously good things, I now believe we Canadians are somehow blunted, spiritually blanched by an excessive emphasis on niceness. Needless to say the idea that Canadians are "nice" is a cliché on the order of "all Americans are loud" or "the French are always rude." So let me be more specific and defining. In "Elegies in Stone" I argued that one of the virtues of Canadian self-effacement is that it pulls the pedestal out from under the colossus of patriotic heroism and encourages a healthy irreverence towards the glories of blood and soil. But writing demands along with humility a kind of arrogance, and it demands that they coexist, so that writers may be humbly receptive to everything around and within them, while at the same time having the toughness to face the world's indifference or rejection. To hold fast to that rejected vision. To see themselves, in their art, as a majority of one.

The kind of "niceness" at issue here is not what Roo Borson has called "radical compassion" — that clear-eyed, unkitschy, passionately active embrace of the world — but something more passive, withdrawing, something stemming from a fear of others' opinions and from a natural desire to be liked. A kind of sentimental, artificial, perfunctory kindness that is above all practical, a strategy instead of a principle, a camouflage not an essence. But wear the suit too long and it comes to suit you, as many a lifetime soldier or market analyst attests.

By feigning niceness for too long men and women can douse their vital flame — or turn it into something smouldering, deadly. The spitting fuse that leads to the explosives. The Canadian war crimes in Somalia serve eloquent notice: Canadians are not fundamentally nice any more than the fastidiously polite Japanese. "A man away from home has no neighbours," the Japanese proverb runs, suggesting among other things that politeness and niceness are little more than a kind of social camouflage and when a man peels off that uniform to don another, of khaki, and finds himself anonymized in a foreign locale, he may be capable of atrocities — more capable than ever for all the years of repression. And *in*capable of reverent intensity, or "radical compassion," which lie somewhere between the twin extremes of repressive fake niceness and utter barbarism. Twin extremes, related, just as sentimentality is tails to the heads of cynicism: extremes corresponding like negative and positive poles.

So artificial "niceness" implies a dangerous imbalance and over time snuffs out the vital flame, or turns the flame to a slow fuse. For women especially this fear of self-assertion can be enervating — and a handicap at times of physical crisis — but for men it's deformative too. As a male writer I came to fear that the narrowness of my vocal range far exceeded my natural limitations, that there were high and low notes of power and honesty I wasn't hitting and might never hit because an ingrown habit of self-effacement and politeness was muting out the high tenor modes of full passion or the bass rumblings of authentic anger. And if they were lost, so was my real voice.

By narrowing a writer's range, niceness has a levelling, homogenizing effect, and makes one voice sound much like another.

Gradually I came to believe in a more forceful, spontaneous approach to life and to writing. Livelier and less careful. Not violent or harsh or unkind, but not "nice" either. And because we live and write in a society that a psychotherapist or self-help book might label passive-aggressive — a society where anger is insufficiently or inauthentically vented, a society where frankness is shunned because it tends to provoke ostracism and thus incur solitude, a society where, to quote another Japanese proverb, "the nail that sticks up gets hammered down" — I've come to aspire to directness and intensity. To love and kindness, yes, but always tipped with fire.

I've failed. At times I've come close — come closer with time — and still failed. Always will fail. Though my books are better than I am.

Still, trying your best to live and write with this fiery

compassion means gradually coming into focus as yourself — a selfish project on the face of it, sure, but how else to lend your community the hybrid vigour and richness and vitality it deserves without being authentically yourself?

This has everything to do with writing, and especially new writing. Like any editor who keeps at it for a while — for me it was six years at *Quarry Magazine* — I grew harder to surprise and delight than I'd been at the start, and at the same time, facing the latest month's bale of manuscripts, I wanted more than ever to be surprised and delighted. To be riveted, challenged. To be changed. For me that's what it boiled down to, a desire to be changed — maybe not in some fundamental way, since in a life you only encounter a handful of books that do that, but in the subtle, lasting way a good poem will change forever how you see that "toddler in the autumn leaves" or that kitchen sink. The way a story that "stays read" will replay itself in the subconscious over and over and become a part of your own experience as if you'd seen or lived the events yourself. As in fact you have. All good art implies the same passionate injunction as that sonnet by Rilke where Apollo is the muse — "for here," the poem ends, "there is no eye / That does not see you. You must change your life."

Not to suffer change is to choose life in the suburbs of the heart. Life, that is, in the shallow, tepid end of the pool. Adult readers have the right to expect and demand that writers not condescend to them but treat them with respect — challenge them, unsettle them, refuse to talk down to them. Personally I don't want false comfort. I don't want to read writers who flop in to join me in the shallow end where, like most people, I sometimes find myself cowering out of fatigue or disappointment or the natural human aversion to spiritual deep waters. I want to read writers like Franz Kafka or Mary Shelley or Mavis Gallant or Cormac McCarthy who grab me by the hair and haul or pitch me out into the deep end of the pool and say Swim, you bastard, your life depends on it.

One thing you can be sure of with writers like that, the ones who compel instead of cosseting you, the ones who treat you like an equal: they'll be out there in the deep waters along with you, you won't be alone.

At *Quarry Magazine* I sometimes did come across new work that changed my life, but much of the time I found myself wading through new stuff the muses hadn't even brushed up against. The writers never called them down. Or up. And often these writers were undeniably talented, gifted, yet the work itself was too often marked by a bland, facile proficiency and as I read I got the feeling the gift had been refused, or ignored, or incarcerated and starved — at any rate pared to a sliver of itself.

Such gifts die quickly in writers lamed by niceness into writing poems and stories that seek to beg favour and befriend the reader, to audition for the reader, to sell themselves and buy off the reader's critical faculties instead of just performing as themselves, like the bird in the Hopkins poem: "what I sing is Me; / For this I came." Or, to give the lines a modern, mean-street spin, "There. Take me or leave me."

Many blame the so-called Creative Writing Workshop Industry for levelling out the uniqueness of promising writers and rationalizing their gifts — and though much can be gained from taking a few basic courses and working with a sympathetic teacher, there is a real danger in conditioning students to accept criticism by committee, or by consensus, as often occurs in the workshop. Flannery O'Connor, a fiercely unique deep-end writer if there ever was one, did attend workshops and still emerged with her own voice. As have others. Still, a rising proportion of the work coming in to *Quarry* from creative writing students — a rapidly growing constituency among those who submit to magazines and those who publish first books — showed evidence of the kind of consensual levelling you'd expect an institutional system to produce. More and more I read a kind of generic workshop story that was difficult to reject yet impossible to remember. Because while workshops can give students a good and useful grounding in the basics (which is all anyone has the right to ask, or expect), they can do little to offset the social conditioning that so often snuffs out the vital spark and precious, redemptive eccentricity in each student, each citizen.

It's not just niceness either. Niceness is one culprit, here in Canada, but Canada is part of a larger, media-malnourished world where the temper of the times is a jeering, fuck-you detachment, and that attitude snuffs the spark as well, replacing it with the facile cleverness that too often passes for true intelligence and too often usurps true feeling. More than ever Canadian writers are torn from the heart's true centre towards one of two lifeless poles: a home and native extreme of well-meaning sentimentality or the bitter antarctic wastes of the mediaworld, with its cult of heartless, unremitting irony. How can a workshop possibly guard a student against the intense gravitation of the poles? Or from commuting manically between them? Perhaps a few can, if the instructor is wise enough and the chemistry and communal spirit of the group sufficiently vital, but for the most part workshops can instill only the method of writing, not the magic and the madness — nor a fierce sense of moral conviction to counter the niceness on the one hand and the anomie on the other. Most new writers will have to have those things already or discover them on their own.

Yet it seems second nature in this institutional age to look to institutions and committees to solve our problems. Some problems can be tackled that way, but the growth of one's writing — one's voice — is indivisibly bound up with the growth of the soul, and committees are no help there. The truth is, our excessive insistence on niceness here in Canada is merely facilitating and aggravating a malaise that's increasingly global. The muses and the magic are not just absent here, they're endangered throughout the so-called First World and their disappearance is linked to the accelerating decline in individuality and individual thought. You don't need to be a conspiracy theorist to see that governments and burgeoning multinationals have a vested interest in levelling out individuality and diversity wherever they find it, and in rendering all of us dull, decent, sedated consumers. Compliant. Nice.

In Mexico City after NAFTA the streets may bear the same names, but how can "angels" or "muses" survive in "the cold soul of [a] city / blown empty by commerce"?

McLuhan promised us a global village. We're getting a global suburb instead.

Because of its origins in and emphasis on the organic world, with its anarchic and inexhaustibly diverse forms and energies, the poetic imagination is subversive of institutions and standardizing monopolies and always has been. So that we need the muses and the angels now more than ever. When diversity of thought and personality and expression — diversity of soul — are crushed among the bureaucratic, conformative structures of a more and more centralized world, the imagining soul, which feeds on freedom and variety, starves and lapses into silence.

There is not much new writing that seems to resist this trend towards generic standardization. Much of it seems to be the work of talented writers whose inner fires have been so banked by the protocol of niceness on the one hand and, on the other, the ironizing abstractions of a multinational world, that they no longer have the energy or inclination to summon the muses whose absence George Bowering laments.

The M in those spreading new mbanx signs, Bob Dylan's collaboration notwithstanding, represents anything but the muse. And in lieu of the hybrid vigour of a society whose citizens venture into the deep end of their own hearts and struggle to become more fully themselves — unique — we have sprawling subdivisions of duplicate grey houses where souls — make no mistake about it — are dying.

A nation can't survive without order and civility but it can't flourish either, ever, without some disorder and passion. Today, because older Canadian writers offer examples and helping hands and because of the abundance of creative writing programs, new Canadian writing shows more promise and competence than ever before, but the conformative pressures of the global suburb will go on subverting those things unless magic and madness — what George Bowering might call the contribution of the muse — become a bigger part of our vision.

The Canadian poet Margaret Avison sang from the deep end over thirty years ago that "For everyone / The swimmer's moment at the whirlpool comes." It could be that for individual writers, for this society, and for the world itself, that moment is fast approaching. Surely there's still a place "mysterious, and more ample," as Avison promised at the end of her poem?

But no Avenue of Angels in the suburbs of the heart.

# 9

# Body Found in Reservoir

*Puritan America, the Human War, &*
*Quentin Tarantino's* Reservoir Dogs

ON A BITTERLY COLD WEEKNIGHT late last fall, I stood hunched, hands pocketed against the weather, in front of an electronics shop on Princess Street. Looking in through the display window at a battery of television screens, three high and four across, I might have seemed to a passerby to have mistaken the glowing window for a source of comfort and warmth. I can't remember exactly what was on. Hockey or football on one of the sets, a made-for-TV movie on another. Commercials, sitcoms. None of it unusually violent, or graphically sexual, yet as I walked off up the street this phrase surfaced in my mind: violence is the sexuality of America.

I couldn't say at first what the words meant, not exactly, but I sensed — as with a line of poetry that rings true even while it resists clear explanation or paraphrase — that there was something to it. Then a few weeks later, after seeing Quentin Tarantino's *Reservoir Dogs*, the phrase recurred to me and in the harsh, rending light of that film its meaning seemed to leap clear. In fact the film casts its third-degree light on a number of questions because in *Reservoir Dogs*,

Tarantino — wittingly, instinctively, or accidentally — frames a parable of our times and our culture in what may be their terminal phase; *Reservoir Dogs* is an elegy for North American sexuality and for the human body itself.

Violence is the sexuality of white North America because violence is all we have left. The passions demand a physical outlet but in our bones we feel it's somehow wrong to love the body. So sex — no matter how aggressively marketed or universally portrayed, no matter how frankly and coolly discussed on talk shows or in the narcotic literature of self-help — remains fraught with an obscure gloom and guilt.

In her essay "Dealing With What's Dealt" (reprinted, from the U.S. quarterly *Salmagundi*, in both *Harper's* and *Brick*) Nancy Huston expands on the idea that perniciously deviant behaviours, like pedophilia and rape, increase rather than disappear where sexual strictness and repression increase. Although the idea is hardly new, it's worth recalling that before this century it would have struck an enormous majority of North Americans as ridiculous and depraved — and that today, though the dubious majority is smaller, it remains a majority. Huston goes on to suggest, rightly, that in North America (as compared, in her essay, to France, where she lives) most people have an ambivalent and basically neurotic relationship with their bodies. While Huston does exempt African-Americans from this continental indictment, there are many other minorities she neglects to mention, all of whom have viewed and treated the body and sexuality in a different way from what I'll call for convenience the founding immigrants. But as applied to this last group her view is roughly valid — which is all you can really ask or expect of such a sprawling generalization.

White North America was founded on fallen bodies — White, Native, African, and Asian. The primal exigencies and physical demands of settlement in the New World dictated that the body be seen at first in a wholly pragmatic way; whether the all-too-visible physiques of the "savages" or the laboriously layered bodies of the settlers themselves, for purposes of survival they had to be harnessed, ordered, enlisted, or enslaved. Or wiped out. So it must have seemed.

But this violently utilitarian approach to the physical life was hardly a matter of grudging adaptation; in fact it was already encoded in the moral cosmology of the settlers, who in the thirteen colonies were largely Puritan, or at least Protestant, and who were leaving an Old World they saw as libertine and debased. It's easy to imagine how the Puritans' standing contempt for physical passions would have been deepened by encounters with the natives, whose semi-nakedness (at least in summer) and "savage" ways would have seemed a challenge to the new community's worldview — a first Temptation in the Wilderness, firming up the settlers' resolve to squelch any hints of paganry in or among themselves. Survival in so exotic and exacting a world, it must have seemed, demanded the unwavering maintenance of social order — of popular conformity and coherence — so that the body, long equated through myth, poetry, scripture, and sermon with the kind of bestial, "untamed" wilderness that ringed the stockades, would have loomed as even more of a threat. A kind of fifth column, chronically mutinous and calling for tough-minded, unceasing invigilation; calling for witches' bodies burning at the stake, the pillars of smoke above them a forecast of the vast arcs of effluent soon to billow up from the factory stacks of Jersey and Lowell and Pittsburgh . . .

For all the virtues of the early settlers — endurance, courage, the dogged egalitarianism and self-reliance they imported from the Old World and which finally bloomed into revolution and democracy — they did plant on the edge of the "virgin wilderness" the seeds of a noxious and perennial dualism, a suspicion of all things organic and carnal, a fear of the passions and a hatred of sex. White North America was founded on fallen bodies, and foundations — as with the settler's house abandoned to the forest, only the cellar and the basestones left — never quite vanish. They just get layered over, harder to see. So despite the outwardly permissive atmosphere of late-twentieth century North America the body is still the enemy, and more than ever, on the street or in the cinema, it gets its just desserts.

On the screen every death is a verdict. This is especially true of American film, which is generally more violent than Canadian film partly because the sociocultural sensibility of the States is basically Old Testament, with its emphasis on righteous judgement and retaliation, an eye for an eye, while the Canadian temper is more New Testament, and liberal. (The attitudes of the two countries to capital punishment bear out this difference most graphically.) Still, when it comes to the Fall — the Old Testament lapsing of the body into shame and disgrace — the countries form a Puritanical common front, the story of Adam and Eve's forcible eviction from paradise and their scramble for raiment standing as the primordial, formative "event" in the culture's psychic history. And whether the violent repercussions are unremitting, as in much American film, or occasional, as in Canadian, the fall of every character on screen is an echo and a judgement, the body punished for its stubborn *bodiness*.

Among other things, violence in the West is an expression of the mind's frustration with the mortal limits of the body, the constraints it lays on the Faustian ambitions of the will.

It does feel somehow right to mistrust the body, to speak of its betraying us when illness or fatigue undermine the will's conquistadorial plans, to see it as the mind's private transit system instead of a worthy end in itself. And if violence is a declaration of hatred, so is a lot of porn, where joyous uncomplicated sexuality is seldom depicted and an air of desperation and frantic exhibitionism, or even a dutiful puritanical doggedness, hang over the proceedings. Or violence, sexual violence.

Violence is not only an expression of our hatred of the body but, whether in art or in schlock, a kind of consecration of it — a ritual celebration. Or even a ritual re-enactment. So the Fall into mortality of Adam and Eve, our psychic parents, is echoed in the mortal "falls" of countless slain characters on the screen or of real people in the street. As if we're condemned to endless recapitulations of a parental sin, a primitive and mindless playing out of some ritual whose meaning is long since forgotten.

But where is the priest or minister to preside over this ceremony of long-lost innocence? As we'll see, *Reservoir Dogs* is a showcase for a kind of new, sacrificial priesthood; as for the old one, its increasing absence is partly an extension of an older half-absence, a carnal absence. Traditionally the priest or minister's body has been hidden under yards and layers of loose heavy cloth, its masculine lineaments disguised, unsexed; in the first settlements of the New World the haunting absence of the minister's body was partly symbolic of one of his main duties — to ensure that the bodies of his flock remained likewise hidden, governable, and chaste.

For the first few hundred years, it worked. Nowadays, if North Americans are still fundamentally puritanical, they show as much skin as anyone else — though in this seeming casualness there's a strain of the frantic exhibitionism I mentioned before in regard to porn. No group of people at peace with their bodies could muster such sad, huddled masses of anorexics and bulimics and the world's highest per capita rate of abuse of steroids, sleeping pills, sedatives, and laxatives. And though it may seem incidental or trivial, the use of euphemism is always telling, and the uniquely North American euphemism for using the toilet — *going to the bathroom* (as if to wash and purify the body) — speaks volumes about a fear of the simplest, most natural parts of life.

The white collars and black suits of the doomed gangsters in *Reservoir Dogs* are the vestments of a latter-day clergy common to modern fiction and cinema — from the inescapably Catholic, sex-fearing mobster Pinkie of Graham Greene's *Brighton Rock* to Mr Blonde and Mr Pink of *Reservoir Dogs*, the killers in our century constitute a sort of hieratic last wave, an ecumenical mop-up crew delivering the *coup de grâce* (and, in *Reservoir Dogs*, a kind of extreme unction) to the human body that the practical Puritans sought merely to conceal, control, and transcend.

Hollywood assassins, like the real-life serial killers who fill the pages of the tabloids, are not merely a kind of brutally skewed priesthood, they are the agents of a dying culture that has institutionalized its fear of the body. That the culture in question does punish the killers is beside the point; often enough, and especially in film, we come to see them as heroes of a kind. Writers and directors can feel assured of securing our admiration for "rebels" like Bonnie and Clyde (and their complementary "opposites," like Dirty Harry) because our admiration is less contingent on political feelings about the law and the outlawed as on our inability to resist the charisma of the powerful, especially when they have the power of life and death. Both the establishment hero of an urban cop film and the gunslinging outlaw of a Western are like matadors to whom we toss roses when they overcome the dark menacing bull of the body. So that, paradoxically, Bonnie and Clyde are actually part of the establishment — a psychic establishment in which the killer, the secret agent, the Robocop, Rambo, whatever, are revered the way matadors are revered: because of their power to destroy the beast, the horned devil — what we fear and hate in ourselves.

Little wonder then that Puritan America has led the world's drive over the last few centuries towards techno-utopias where the body will be transcended, made obsolete, refined out of existence. The technologies that have paved the way for cyberspace, and the further disembodiment of "cyber-sex," are ensuring that "virtual realities" will continue to oust visceral realities at a hyped-up postmodern pace. And as the life of the body continues to recede along with manual work and natural surroundings, or to be compartmentalized into lunch-hour workouts on StairMasters, Virtual Cliffsides, or digitized treadmills in video-filled gyms, our appetite for cinematic violence — for a vicarious physical life of challenge, danger, and extremes — will keep on building. Meanwhile each killing, in the pages of a novel or in the backstreets of Toronto, consolidates and finalizes the body's denial.

Violence is the sexuality of America because it's the outlet and consummation our longings are all channelled towards.

In the film *Reservoir Dogs* what is ultimately most striking is the absence of women. In this vividly realized postmodern tragedy, women, with one brief exception, exist in a "virtual" way alone — in the conversation and crude physical jokes the killers exchange over their diner breakfasts minutes before hitting a wholesale diamond outlet, in occasional other remarks the men make about women they've known, and in the account we later get of the robbery, where several women clerks are shot dead. We never get a good look at who has served the killers in the diner, though we hear it's a woman, and at one point a classically beehived diner waitress can be glimpsed faintly in the background, her back to the camera. Meanwhile the men discuss the ethics of tipping, only Mr Pink demurring at the general consensus that a hardworking gal deserves her fifteen percent. This a few minutes before the robbery and slaughter.

As for the bodies of the murdered women, they're never seen at all. In fact the shooting spree in the wholesale outlet is the one important scene we never get a glimpse of, in flashback or otherwise — a surprising omission which makes the bodies of the slain clerks especially significant, and in a sense present to the eye of the imagination. The deaths are mentioned, either with moral disgust, professional disapproval, or amused indifference, by Mr White, Mr Pink, and the actual killer, Mr Blonde, respectively, but the bodies are entirely "disappeared." Given the expectation primed in the viewer by serial flashbacks that gradually fill in the story's blanks and seem to be building towards the big, primordial blank — ground zero, the violent, pivotally dramatic "fall" of the robbery — this is a brilliant directorial move.

One woman actually does appear in the film. She is on screen for just a few blurred, turbulent seconds — long enough to get shot in her car by Mr Orange, who is in fact an undercover cop. (Mr White and Mr Orange are trying to steal her car after the robbery; she pulls a pistol from the glove compartment and shoots Mr Orange, who automatically

responds.) So that a representative of "law and order," supposedly planted to defend not only the rights of proprietors
but the bodies of citizens, is liable for the shooting of the
one woman to appear on screen. The fact that Mr Orange
has shot the woman against his will, so to speak, only adds
to the sense that things are out of control, rolling on with
their own momentum — that the war on the body recruits
and uses us all, willing or not. And clearly the war is an allied
effort. Clint Eastwood's outlaw Jesse Wales and Eastwood's
lawman Dirty Harry meet in the undercover Mr Orange —
a trinity of heroes in the holy war, the dirty "human war"
that Ginsberg accused America of waging.

The scene is important for a second reason: its suggestion
of a grotesquely skewed sexuality. In a contorted echo or a
savage punchline to the dirty jokes told in the diner an hour
before, the undercover cop and the woman exchange gun-
fire from inches apart, with a terrible intimacy — a kind
of ballistic intercourse in which each fires a single round
into the other's guts. This confrontation sensationally en-
capsulates the brute realities of Western sexuality as the
millennium ends — the impossibility of trust in a time of
sexual plague, the vexed, desperate nature of the contemporary male-female embrace, the ongoing wounding or killing
of unloved bodies. We're never told whether the woman lives
or dies.

As Mr White says in an earlier scene, of a woman he once
worked with, "You don't want to push that man-woman
thing too far." Or, it seems, too close.

Yet there are closer embraces here. If you can call them
that. Grapplings, maybe. In Tarantino's grim portrait of
postmodern America, sexuality is reduced to the locker room
wrestling of two thugs in a posh office where the fatal
hold-up is being planned, the brief and horrible lapdance

of Mr Blonde as he clutches and mutilates a chair-bound hostage, and, finally and remarkably, the embrace of two bleeding, dying men, Mr White and Mr Orange — the law and the outlawed, drawn together and equated in the end. Because in the film's final minutes the freshly wounded Mr White, who has figured as the only one of the gang to show any humane scruples, crawls towards the undercover cop, Mr Orange, and maternally cradles his head and blood-soaked upper body. When Mr Orange confesses that he's a cop — and despite the hair-trigger warnings of the SWAT team that has just burst into the warehouse — Mr White shoots him, is then shot himself, and the screen goes dark. So the film ends on the obliteration of its one spark of human light, human contact reduced to a few seconds of feeble comforting before the cops-and-robbers action reflares momentarily and the curtain falls.

That the only real flesh-to-flesh contact in *Reservoir Dogs* involves men, that all the men seem to live alone, unattached, and that women are virtually absent or invisible, will surely lead some to perceive a strong homoerotic subtext in the film. I have to admit I can't see it. *Reservoir Dogs* is neither homoerotic nor heteroerotic but rather anti-erotic — a film not about Eros but about the murder of Eros, its vivisection and disappearance.

A long time ago I wrote, in a failed poem, "No man can fear God and love women." I was writing about religious fanatics and fundamentalists, and trying to suggest, I think, that when a pious fear of God involves the believer in a hierarchy where men cower in the shadow of a "jealous God," and women stand lower than men, the highest kind of human love — love based on equality and respect, not on fear and possession — is hardly apt to bloom. But there was more to it than that. To fear God is to believe that humanity is abject, unworthy, and fallen, that the abstract realm of spirit, sky, and mind is superior to earthly carnal life and not born of it; to fear God is to buy the old dualist line, to see the body as a trammel and a cross to bear instead of the donor of consciousness, the giver of the gift. And where the body and its gifts are disrespected, so are women — not only on account of Eve, set up to take the fall in Eden, but because women's bodies are the source of all bodies, the basic physical well-spring. *No man can fear God and love women.* The line is portentous, it has an archaic feel to it, a kind of undergraduate stridency, and it's grossly presumptuous — as if my theories on who can love and who can't are sufficient to the complex refractory nature of love in the world. Yet there is a grain of truth there. And if I'd remembered the line on that night last fall, walking away from that battery of TV screens, the words *violence is the sexuality of America* surfacing in my thoughts, it might have served as a key to decode them.

The two lines came to me years apart, but they go together. In the years in between, I've been trying to write and live my way into an understanding of what love means in a culture where fear and hatred are the high-octane fuels rocketing us through Faustian exploits of expansion, conquest, and increase. As if we might thereby escape the limits of the body. Escape its mortality as well. The crowd in the cockpit will never understand the lyrical insight that it's death and its mortal decrease that make love and beauty possible; beauty is a function of transience, and without death human love could not be.

So how are we to love in a time when our bodies are disappearing? Being disappeared? No one can love only in the abstract, in the head. As people know who've tried to will themselves into loving someone they feel they ought to love, but don't, real love is not a conceptual thing. Love is cellular. Even "Platonic" love. So that wherever the flesh is hated, or endangered, love is threatened as well. The body's ongoing abduction — witch trial, summary execution, gangland driveby — means all of us have been born into a war zone, a place of chalk silhouettes and Hiroshima leaf-shadows, with the bodies gone and Eros reduced to a few images in the rubble: An ad hoc madonna with a pale, parodic Christ in his arms, both killers, both dying; a man and a woman fumbling inches apart, as if frantic to shed their clothing for a unifying, Edenic embrace, but able in the end to touch and inter-penetrate only with steel and lead.

# 10

# Firing Line

*Consistency is the hobgoblin of little minds.*
— Emerson

OVER THE LAST DECADE AND A HALF much has been said about the small-c conservative thought of "conservative intellectuals," and if the thoughts and the thinkers themselves are often under attack, the terms they go by remain unchallenged. Yet the very idea of "conservative thought" is a flagrant contradiction in terms.*

I'm not questioning the merit of individual conservative thoughts — thoughts stressing, for example, the conservation of some of the ideals and principles that have developed, often with great struggle, over the last few thousand years. Surely conservative thoughts are justified when it comes to the right of the accused to be presumed innocent and to be

---

* By "conservative thought" I mean not only the opinions of rightists in Canada and elsewhere, but thought that aims to conserve the status quo in any country, whether right- or left-wing. By this definition someone of almost any political stripe could be, or become, a "conservative thinker."

tried before a jury of peers instead of a posse or an inquisition. But to examine the way the legal system actually works, day to day, is to recognize it as defective and in need of change. So that it's possible to have conservative thoughts about some basic principles or elements of a flawed system, but given that a system is flawed (all systems are flawed) it should not be possible to think conservatively about it as a whole. Unless, of course, you have a vested interest in maintaining the flaws. In which case you're not thinking, but scheming.

Thought, by its primary definition, is not a matter of fixed opinion or of prejudice but of ongoing, organic process, so that by definition true thought — the exploration of ideas and issues — can never be static or conservative. In a Utopia, conservatism would be the only sensible philosophy, but Utopia, like Eden, is a figment, a cop-out, a reified nostalgia projected safely into the future or the past.

As citizens of a (blessedly) imperfect world we have no choice but to go on exploring.

I was talking over some of these ideas with a man I know, an eloquent "young conservative" (by rights another oxymoron), and he objected on a number of grounds. Surely, he shook his head, surely I couldn't deny that some conservative thinkers — William F. Buckley, Jr., for example — were highly intelligent? And I agreed that I could hardly deny it, Buckley is very bright.

But does that mean that he *thinks*? As Edward de Bono and others have pointed out, a powerful mind can become not only a moral liability but a mental one; many brilliant thinkers grow so proud of their fine-tuned logical apparatus, so accustomed to verbally checkmating others and seeming right, so spoiled by the deference or acquiescence of mental "inferiors," that they stop exploring ideas with the kind of self-reflexive, self-interrogating intensity they're capable of and perhaps exercised when younger.

Often, as de Bono suggests, people with less brilliant, more patient minds make better thinkers, and he points out how "slower" minds, like slower walkers, tend to see more of the landscape. What he fails to explore is the way intellectuals sometimes outsmart and subvert themselves through arrogance, how feelings of pride and smug superiority will always separate thinkers from the world they pretend to penetrate and explain — so that many a brilliant mind has scrambled up the ladder of intellectual pride into a heaven of abstractions while other, less dazzling thinkers have kept both feet on the ground. Which is the first and final plane of wisdom, the place all theories and datums start from and finally fall back to, like stages of a rocket or a satellite: means to the greater end of human knowledge, not ends in themselves.

I put it to my friend that Buckley is surely intelligent by any standard definition, but he's no thinker and doesn't deserve to be called an intellectual. Essentially he's a skilled and nimble rhetorician who forges airtight arguments with a discernible agenda in mind. Like any conservative thinker he supports a specific ideology — and the party that embodies it — and he generously sets at its disposal his considerable mental gifts.

But "gifts" has a benevolent connotation that's out of place here. What I'm saying is that Buckley, and many others like him, retool their minds into weapons instead of what they might become — ploughshares, breaking new ground and raking to the surface unexpected finds. Such conservative "thinkers" do not think when a new issue arises — they react, like armed and frightened men. Or, to vary the metaphor, they feed each new datum into a rigidly programmed mental computer, and the data, no matter how dissonant, is duly neutralized, assimilated, brought to heel. The commentary that eventually issues from their lips (or your lips, my lips, since everyone engages in conservative thought at times) has been automatically processed and stripped of all mental freshness and spontaneity. The computer in question is lodged in the heart of a map-filled war room, or a poorly camouflaged high-tech tank. No wonder Buckley calls his show *Firing Line*.

Obviously there's no shortage of left-wing thinkers whose brains have been likewise enlisted and automatized; only the software differs. If I have slightly more sympathy for the left-wing ideologues it's because the principles they use their intelligence to promote are more generous and decent and theoretically of benefit to many, not just to a limited class. Buckley and others like him know where their bread is buttered and have dedicated their intellectual lives to defending a status quo that benefits and privileges them. Conversely a Marxist from, say, the British aristocracy has nothing material to gain and much to lose should fundamental social change ever occur (though of course he or she may simply be after power in the new dispensation). Still, it's hard not to see and admire a kind of selflessness in the Marxist's stance, even if the ideology itself, like all ideologies, is reductive and impracticable.*

But is Buckley afraid only of losing the privileges of wealth? Surely there's more to right-wing conservative

---

* Is it cynical to observe that many of the people who attach themselves to causes are bandwagon radicals, and that many "privileged" radicals are encouraged by the knowledge that fundamental social change probably will not occur — that they'll be able to have their cause and dine out on it too?

thought than that. I told my conservative (*Progressive* Conservative) friend that I had the suspicion, odd as it might sound, that Buckley is afraid of dying.

My friend rolled his eyes. "We're all afraid of dying."

"But some more than others," I said.

Fear of chaos, of randomness, of the essential inconstancy of organic life are part and parcel of the human inheritance, the shadow-side of our birthright. Small wonder that many, haunted by the fear of death — which grows with age and is honed further in our rootless world by the loneliness of unbelonging — feel a visceral tug, as if on some phantom umbilicus, towards a paradise of order and certainty, a place beyond change, decay, and the ambient chaos of modern life. Observation suggests that most of us crave, sometimes or constantly, a sort of terminal order, a destination beyond worry, fatigue and entropy, rising crime- and interest-rates, the general sense of galloping disintegration.

The hunger for certainty is as human as the hunger for love. And in recent years the growth of fundamentalism in various forms — religious, political, scientific, nationalist — has reflected a growing need and pandered to it. The allure of fascism in the thirties was precisely that it promised, in a time of upheaval and fragmentation, to inaugurate a new Heroic Age of forcefulness and order where the trains would run on time, where all citizens would share the same wholesome purpose and values, and where everyone would feel and look like members of one vast extended family. As Martin Amis wrote in his *New Yorker* review of Philip Larkin's *Collected Letters*, people, especially in times of crisis, do have a natural preference for "the familiar and the familial." But "natural" or not, this deeply conservative fear of change and of strangers, with its correlative urge for perfect order — this hankering after Edens and Heroes —

is radically anti-human and self-defeating, since people do change and are inevitably imperfect.

Despite the romantic blood and soil demagogy of fascist regimes, fascism feeds at the deepest level on a *fear* of blood and soil — fear of the genuine body and the actual earth, not their poetic idealizations. And if a terror of the organic lies at the static heart of fascism, then the worship of the machine that characterized the ideology and art of totalitarian Europe in the thirties was an expression not of reverence but of fear. (So in fascist as well as Stalinist iconography the cold, gleaming, monolithically efficient machine figured as the god presiding over all future Edens. Humankind must strive to remake itself in the image of that god, that idol. So the Nazi athlete was revered not only for being more exaltedly human, an Übermensch, but for being more like a machine.)

How little things have changed.

Conservatism's fear of the organic — fear of the body, and detachment from it — flags itself most blatantly in the support of right-wing (and conservative left-wing) fundamentalists for mass censorship and book bannings, on sexual grounds. And in their opposition to sex education in the schools. And in their support for capital punishment, carried out by way of various expensive and ingenious machines — the ultimate expression of a state's contempt for individual human life.

Conservative thought, whether in Beijing or in Barrie, Ontario, betrays a fundamental mistrust in humanity, which it portrays as fallen ("There were giants in the earth in those days," but now . . .), riddled with flaws, requiring a kind of paternal superintendency and the imposition of a stern, coercive order. The people I would call true or organic thinkers refuse to see human beings as either debased and fallen from some primordial playground or as perfectible and angelic; neither the stinking denizens of a Hieronymus Bosch hallucination nor the sweet, beaming townsfolk of a Norman Rockwell.

True thought is essentially *realistic* insofar as the mutability, fluidity, and interconnection of all things, which it takes as its grounding tenets, have been increasingly borne out this century by the work of quantum mechanics and nuclear physics. Conservative thought — dualistic, hierarchical, normative, and static — is based instead on neurotic, if natural, misconceptions.

So how does this "true, organic thought" actually function in the world? For one thing, real thinkers do their best to maintain or further their intellectual autonomy, to stay free of all the calcified theories, creeds, clubs, and institutions that seek to constrain and reduce thought to a set of inflexible norms. Clearly this effort involves a constant self-interrogation over assumptions long since internalized and always present, subliminally, always hobbling true thought — but though such "received ideas" always will be there in some form, the effort to identify them, and the awareness it brings, are significant.

Intellectual autonomy doesn't mean that true thinkers won't sometimes praise or back a particular political view or party; in the world as it is such choices are a necessary evil. But as Julia Kristeva suggests, even if true thinkers put their support, for now, behind Party X, they maintain a critical detachment and are willing to applaud the opposition if one of their policies seems more sensible or humane. And if they're involved in politics they probably spend most of their time trying to change or improve the system instead of just supporting one party or another.

Those who aspire to organic thought refuse to view any of their opinions as final. Difficult though it is — because the heart's dark side will always crave certainty and terminal order — they have to admit that their ideas are really hypotheses, always tentative, always relative, almost always subject to change. But besides a few basic axioms (would anyone honestly contend that torture is not evil?) the true thinker can't be sure of anything and must have the courage — the "negative capability," to paraphrase Keats — not to grope after false certainties or the fundamentalism that lead so often to dogma and death.

# II

# A Wild Peculiar Joy

A FEW YEARS AGO a friend in Toronto sent me a story he'd written, along with a note saying that it had just been rejected by a literary magazine and would I mind having a look at the story, because the editor's comment made no sense to him. Too reverent, the editor had decided. The tone of your story is too reverent.

Some stories surely are too "reverent" — pious and portentous, bombastic, overwrought — but I liked the tone of my friend's story and I told him so. Still, the damage had been done and for a while he could only write stories that were conventionally modern — witty, hip, quirky, and urban; streetwise. Nothing wrong with that, except there are plenty of streetwise Big City writers at work already and more to the point, his adopted tone wasn't him. The new stories were all right but they were nothing special — nothing out of the ordinary, I mean. I found myself wishing that he had kept on taking risks with big emotions and grappling with great themes.

As I said, this all happened some time ago but I've been thinking about it again because these days, it seems, my friend is lapsing back into his old unfashionable ways and it's a relief to me — partly because I think he's writing authentically again, sure, but mainly (how unsurprising) for a more selfish reason. The reason, of course, is that as a writer he was doing and is now again doing what I've been trying to do all along — and every crowd loves to grow, and even those writers who like to see themselves as renegades crying solo in the wilderness need to feel somehow ratified, vindicated by the efforts of others.

I envied my friend the wording of his rejection, if not the rejection itself, because like the man in Philip Larkin's poem "Church Going" I kept surprising within myself "a need to be more serious." More *reverent*. There had been a time when I, like him — and for similar reasons — did my best to bury that sense of earnest wonder and existential respect on which I felt all theory and action should be based; but the "reverence" proved more resilient than I could have foreseen. All of us, I came to believe, nurse a secret fund of it deep inside and say nothing because reverence is unfashionable, anachronistic, the sensibility of another time, whether in our lives or the world's; when the culture was young, or we were. Life in society has always involved us in an elaborate, baroquely choreographed charade, but now instead of just hiding our feelings we try to hide the fact that we have them at all — or watch others vomit them out on talk shows, shamelessly, all our pent-up poisons seemingly channelled through them, those sad-sack Warholites whoring for their fifteen minutes. Seconds. Cynicism, sentimentality — the pendulum, as in any time of fragmentation, tracing a manic arc from one extreme to the other, never pausing at the meridian of balance.

This, as everybody knows firsthand, is an age of glibness and facile wit, of sarcasm, barbed irony, of nihilism force-fed to us as pragmatism and realism and listen, kid, it's a dog eat dog world. But while reverence is surely a better place to live — an Eldorado of freshness and energy — it's a trouble spot as well; if that were not the case we'd all be cartwheeling in its meadows instead of buttressing our flesh-and-bone forts and bunkers on the shadow-side of the stream.

For one thing it's vital to distinguish between reverence — a willingness to be awed by the world and to express that sense of wonder and respect, even if it means being laughed at — and naïveté. Maintaining a sense of reverence in a world poisonous with chemical and moral toxins demands courage and a kind of inspired obstinacy; naïveté, on the other hand, will always be reckless, foolhardy, and self-negating. The world is full of pitfalls and predators and while the reverential can detect and avoid them and still celebrate life, the naïve and the credulous are soon swallowed. Still, the logical, binary habits of thought enforced by language drive us to assume that if people are earnest and reverent they must be short on skepticism and *ir*reverence — and since it would be dangerous and stupid to view advertisers or most politicians and corporate lawyers with anything but skepticism, "reverence" again smacks of credulity and the kind of unthinking trust too many people place in technology, say, or in the medical establishment, or in the law of supply and demand.

But reverence can and must be selective. Reverence as I understand it means the courage to admire and praise whatever earns or merits our love, and to struggle to change whatever betrays our trust or proves itself unworthy.

A reverent person believes in human potential and is apt to grant strangers the benefit of the doubt, recognizing that people tend to flourish and yield up their best if their best is what is assumed or expected. So the expectation of the good becomes a kind of self-fulfilling prophecy, in the best sense of the phrase.

Reverence has to be distinguished from mirthlessness as well. Earnestness unleavened with a sense of irony and proportion can be mortally boring, while earnest political enthusiasms can shade or slide lightning-fast into self-righteous, lethal zealotry. William Wordsworth was surely one of the most earnest poets who ever wrote, but although his best work courses with an exhilarating, childlike wonder and rooted enthusiasm, I doubt I'm the only Wordsworth admirer who still feels he would rather have met and dined with, say, Swift, Austen, Byron, Wilde, Stein, or Kerouac. Still, a few years ago Dennis Gentilcore, then a graduate student at Bristol University, wrote his dissertation on "Comedy in Wordsworth," arguing that while the poet's sense of humour is exceedingly subtle, a patient reading of *The Prelude* will reveal a highly refined comic sensibility at work. At one point Dr Gentilcore cites Wordsworth's fanciful comparing of clouds to various creatures — cattle, camels, hedgehogs.

Perhaps we'll be excused for feeling the chief comic sensibility at work here is Gentilcore's.

As for zealots, our century has shown over and over that indiscriminately earnest zeal, no matter how well meant at the outset, leads with apocalyptic rapidity to dictatorship and systematic, or chaotically tribal, mass murder.

In the end, reverence untempered by skepticism and self-doubt is as dangerous as the most cynical misanthropy.

Which brings things back to the present day, and the place we're at now. The pat nihilism of films like *Batman* (which *Rolling Stone* astutely called "the first film of the nineties") seems symptomatic of this Age of Clowns, which wears a joker's mask or a fuck-off face to hide its despair, its disillusion, its bewildered anomie. Our society seems more and more like a kind of latch-key kid — hip, tough, and wise-cracking on the surface, an angry tormented orphan within. But how else to carry on in the world as it is? Media advances this century ensure that most of us are chronically shell-shocked from a daily barrage of horrific news, and the pressures and stresses of day-to-day urban life make it too hard, too taxing to remain emotionally and mentally engaged with the world in any sustained way. The battle rages on too many fronts and the body has limits. Subconsciously overwhelmed, we can do little but retreat into private or virtual realities, relying on the sterile, fugitive discharge of bitter wit to ease the panic, resorting to the slick talk-show repartee that passes for humour these days and helps disguise our growing fear and disgust with the world. As for emotion, when it's not suppressed it tends to be cranked up into talk-show hysterics, or sentimentalized, trivialized in trashy romance novels and made-for-TV films.

Sentimentality, like artificial niceness, is a bowdlerization, a kitschy burlesque of true feeling and has nothing to do with reverence; cynicism, sometimes held up as the opposite of sentimentality, in fact represents the sentimental sickness in its terminal phase (and if this sounds counterintuitive consider the course of German Naziism from the early thirties to the end of the war, or the storied lovingkindness of certain death-camp commandants toward their kittens and lap dogs). In the end, both kitsch and cynicism are the outward signs of a psychic schism, a complementary imbalance in which the world is seen as either daisy-fresh and wholly free of "shit" (to echo Milan Kundera's definition of kitsch) or altogether buried in it, and reeking. Sheer Eden or sulphurous hell. And nothing in between.

When the world seems altogether to have shit itself, the earnest and the reverent among us seem like aliens, or imbeciles. Easy targets. In their prophetic, hieratic guise they ask us to fathom deep waters under the surface of things when we know all the rivers and seas are polluted, dying. They urge us to change our life, to rise and transcend in a New Age atmosphere rife with angels, but the skies are toxic too and full of stealth bombers, spy satellites, and ultraviolet rays. They summon us back to the heart of things but we've come to associate all summonses with litigation, or Big Brother, or the endless Via Dolorosa of deadlines and meaningless duplicate obligations.

But there's something else. They're a reminder — a galling memento — of the intensity we're afraid we've lost. A certain innocence; passion of a certain pitch. Alexander Scala calls youth the Renaissance of a person's life and asks what we might have achieved had we not let the world, which is too much with us, eat away at that Florentine ebullience, freshness, and vitality. The marvellous excess of youth! Its ardour, its exalted sensations! If in Scala's model middle-age is the Age of Industry, then what life-stage does postmodern smarm suggest, both for individuals and the world?

But at least the postmodern sensibility offers the comic relief, the cosmic relief, of humour. Right? Well, yes and no. I think basically there are two kinds of humour, corresponding roughly with the "reverent" and "irreverent" sensibilities: radical, or rooted, humour, and snide humour. Or, to put it another way, serious humour and wit. While "serious humour" may not sound very promising in terms of laughs, some of the funniest people I've met and read are what I would call "serious humorists." Gary Larson's *The Far Side* cartoons are especially interesting and important in this regard because they run counter to most trends in humour these days (although now a number of cartoonists are trying to imitate him, and some, like Dan Pirraro, are doing good work of their own). Of course on one level Larson's cartoons are clearly *ir*reverent — they poke fun at human pride and pretension, as did the original, TV *Batman* in its own campy way — but on another level they're serious and reverent. If there's a moral subtext to Larson's cartoons it's the idea that in the greater scheme of things human beings are not all that important and not all that different from the animals over whom they arrogantly claim "dominion." So that on one level Larson's cartoons suggest the fundamental inter-connectedness of things, which after all is one of the primary insights of the reverent (and religious) sensibility — and the starting point for any child's sense of wonder at the world.

And what about snide humour? Wit? It can be wildly funny, no question, but at the deepest level it betrays a detachment from the world, a rigid and conservative distaste for all things organic and changeable. For *life*. Sarcasm and vicious irony (as opposed to gentle or subtle irony) atomize and objectify the world; snide humour is inherently dualistic and hierarchical, always diminishing the object of laughter and tacitly hailing the joker's superiority. (Some things do call for violent diminution, yet in *A Modest Proposal* Jonathan Swift, by opting for the bizarrely satiric instead of an obvious assault, delivers a far more telling, and lasting, blow against the enemies of the poor.)

The snickering put-down or glib witticism are the easiest ways of *seeming* intelligent.

Ian Watt writes, of Restoration Comedy, "We may smile at the verbal and intellectual brilliance of epigram, but we sense a mocking and even hostile rejection of the objects satirized, and if our emotions are aroused, they tend to be negative — scorn, disgust, hatred." Wit, he continues, "is more exclusively directed to the mind," while humour — what I've called radical or serious humour — "combines appeals to the head and the heart."

But if the terrified irreverence of our Age of Clowns would seem to sound a death knell — of canned laughter — for such "serious humour," it seems also to be fomenting a kind of reverent reaction, a renaissance of passionate and concrete embodied writing and "serious humour" which brings with it the sound of full-bodied laughs. Fiction writers of the new generation like Eliza Clark, Jason Heroux, Gil Adamson, and Caroline Adderson show that those of an engaged and instigated reverence can be funny, often very funny, and at the same time clear-eyed. Open-hearted and streetwise both. The best of the new generation are writers who love people too much to sneer, but know them too well to kitsch them over or touch up their flaws. In a world where the loudest voices are those of demagogues and talk-show hosts with their guilesome moralizing, critics playing games of intellectual Tetris, and the forgers of cynical/sentimental ad campaigns, such voices are a balm: serious and funny, wary but engaged, earnest and yet irreverent — but reverent.

# 12

# Jones

*I was too drunk to notice that it was raining. Because I was drunk, I had confused the rain with tears. The rain ran down Assa's window, and the same rain soaked my hair and clothes. I had been rained on for twenty-one years, but I had never noticed it before. I stood at the end of the driveway, and the rain soaked my hair and my clothes and my skin. I felt the rain on my skin, and it was the same rain that fell on Assa's window, and the same rain that had always fallen. For that moment, I felt like something made of flesh and bone and skin, like something human.*

— Daniel Jones, "The People One Knows"

I

THE LAST TIME I saw Daniel Jones he was standing on the northwest corner of Bloor and Brunswick, in Toronto. This was a year before he took his own life in an apartment not far from that place. It was snowing and windless and the huge flakes were wafting straight down to gather slowly on his hat — the same black beret he'd been wearing the first time I met him, in Kingston, four years before, at a writers' conference. And with the beret and that lost, stalked, ironic expression he was so much the Jones I knew from photographs and the references of friends — and from our one previous meeting — that I almost laughed. I would have laughed but for the man beside me at the wheel of the cab, surly and hunched up, muttering. The light went green and the car bucked forward, the cabbie angling for a left onto Bloor but then holding back; the walk signal was on but Daniel just stood there on the lip of the curb instead of crossing in front of us. The driver made a fist and slammed it on the horn. Daniel kept gazing upward with an oblivious, bereft expression, as if recognizing the face, the silhouette, of an ex-friend or old lover framed in a high window across the way. The Brunswick House Tavern. Or higher up, above the roofline — Daniel eyeing the static of the falling snow and waiting for a clear picture, some meaningful signal, to emerge from the big screen of the sky.

I leaned up against the dash. Daniel remained on the curb like a greying monument as passersby shoved round him, jostling out into Bloor Street and crossing between him and us. I'm no longer sure if I rapped on the windshield or not. It was over so fast — the exasperated driver surging into a gap in the foot-traffic, then braking, skidding, sure that Daniel would lurch from the sidewalk even now; finally tamping the accelerator, cursing as we fishtailed and the rear end slid within a foot of the curb. *Fucking imbecile*, the driver said, but softly, without gusto or conviction and almost, it seemed, by way of apology. The extra few seconds, a few nickels and dimes.

If the window had been open I might have reached out and touched Daniel as we passed — though maybe I've let the cab drift closer to him in memory, its rear wheel spinning through a gutter of slush and slamming into the curb, maybe spattering his army boots, his blue jeans from the knees down. . . . Four years earlier, and a few weeks before I met him for the first time, I'd given my first public reading and I remember how fear and adrenaline had sped up my experience of time, my inner clock not ticking but going off like an alarm. And what a false and paltry alarm it had turned out to be. At the corner of Bloor and Bathurst, Daniel, on the edge of an actual emergency I try now to fathom but never can, seemed to be feeling the opposite — time slowed to an i.v. trickle, or the timeless present of the TV screen after the station leaves the air.

Seconds later when I twisted in my seat and glanced back, Daniel was no longer on the curb. I couldn't find him on the south side of Bloor either, but then visibility was bad, the rear window bleared with dirty slush. When the driver veered north onto Albany I turned back around.

"Fucking guy back there, eh?" The driver looked straight ahead as he spoke. He wore a jaunty new tweed cap pulled rakishly low on his brow, but his face was caved and sallow.

"I know him," I said.

A week later I would receive a cheerful letter from Daniel acknowledging some suggestions I'd made about one of his stories — a story I wanted to use in *Quarry Magazine*. In "Richard's Last Flight" a patently doomed young man aims a scoped automatic rifle at the crowded viewing deck of the CN Tower and asks a friend for further instructions. To pull the trigger, or not to. That scene's moral repercussions still resonate for me, disturbing, like the lingering echoes of a gunshot in the city. . . .

In the same letter Daniel, still upbeat, mentioned that he was hard at work polishing a collection of stories for publication the next spring. But he never just "polished." He rethought, he re-arranged and rewrote, he started over again from scratch. He agonized. Half a year after I accepted "Richard's Last Flight" he was still sending me new versions.

And now, almost two years to the day since his death, as I sit here trying to rethink and revise this piece of my own, I appreciate more than ever his rigour and tenacity, his dedication, the way his consciousness can be felt there on the page, tangibly striving with a savage candour and clear-eyed irony for purity and simplicity of expression. Sometimes, giving walk-on parts to undisguised literary celebrities, he seems coy and offhand, but generally his irony is restrained and mature. Few could have tried harder than Daniel to be honest on the page, and it shows. Of course prose stripped down to the bare essentials in the interests of unadorned, unmannered honesty can itself come to seem mannered — as Hemingway's and Carver's sometimes did — but in the long run a period of paring down can only make a writer tougher, sharper, truer. No way to know for sure how much that decade of paring down took out of Daniel. But surely one of the saddest things about his suicide is that having worked so hard to strip himself naked on the page he was ready to move in a new direction, and he never got the chance. I wish I could have seen where he'd have gone. So I feel now a bit as I felt in the cab, spinning away from the corner where I saw Daniel for the last time — me looking back through the layers of cold, gathering static, trying for a last glimpse.

2

*We live together, we act on, and react to, one another; but*
*always and in all circumstances we are by ourselves. The*
*martyrs go hand in hand into the arena; they are crucified*
*alone. Embraced, the lovers desperately try to fuse their*
*insulated ecstasies into a single self-transcendence; in vain.*
*By its very nature every embodied spirit is doomed to suffer*
*and enjoy in solitude.*
> — Aldous Huxley, *The Doors of Perception*

I FIRST MET DANIEL JONES in Kingston at the Annual
General Meeting of the Canadian Writers' Union, in 1989.
I'd published a first book of poems early that year and had
quickly applied to join the Union — partly hoping, I think,
that it would solidify or strengthen the frail sense of validity
the book had lent me. Yet even as a card-carrying member I
felt like a plagiarist, a fraud.

I've come to see this impostor-feeling as something most
writers share, and not just after a first book — but I could
not have known that then. Local writers like Bronwen Wallace
and Tom Marshall, consistently generous with newcomers,
encouraging yet candid, would have told me the brute truth
if I'd asked, but it hardly seemed credible that they with their
experience and many publications could ever doubt their
validity. Their identity. Or that Daniel could either. *Jones*,
he called himself then, and that blunt, Beat, streetsmart
contraction seemed to broadcast a defiant cockiness — like
someone daring to be known, to be recognized, by Smith. A
*nom de plume*! It was what real writers did. Jones: a single
crisp declarative syllable swaggering with bravado. Jones
sounded cool. He had to be. I knew that in naming his own

book of poems *The Brave Never Write Poetry* he was just being modest, ironic.

I had no notion that I was going to meet him at the AGM because at that time, viewing the world with a clunky, lumbersome lack of subtlety, I would have thought him too much the renegade to join any kind of league. Now I think that few people actually choose the position of full outsider, and those that do are often waiting, hoping, for a suitably sincere invitation to join one group or another. It's true that in the bosom of any group, mainstream or marginalized (the academic clique, the Old Boys' club, the feminist, the ethnic, the regional set) writers may find themselves too cushioned and muffled by mutual approval and other tribal consolations to write their best — to work alone on those unaccommodated margins where all things are urgently at stake. But writers with no community at all can be muffled, or silenced altogether, by harder things. Bitterness, loneliness. Despair. The sense that their words and stories will never resonate in sympathetic ears, that the words are bound to fade out with them, unexpressed and unreceived — unloved — the signal sent out but lost in the static between clearer stations.

At that AGM, Jones was a newcomer like me. And no doubt feeling just as counterfeit. I met him on the last night of the conference, a Saturday, at the party after the "gala banquet."

It took place in a huge low-ceilinged basement under Victoria Hall, the largest student residence at Queen's University, where most of the writers were staying. The basement was dark, the acoustics muted, and though at first the coolness was a bracing change from the humid June heat upstairs and outside, towards the end of the night, despite the dancing, I felt chilled, cut off from the summer, anxious to get back out into the breezy, sweet-scented night air. I never have been able to spend more than a few waking hours in a basement, and though for a while this one had been vitalized by the music, and the booze and the dancing, towards the end, with people drifting back upstairs, the DJ packing up and the coolness seeping into our bones, it had the muffled, sepulchral feel of all basements — as if life in all its sweat and hustle and passionate excess were bustling on somewhere far away, far above. How the buried dead would feel about the world if they could still feel.

I only met Daniel towards the end. As the crowd thinned out I spotted him — knew him from his photograph, that cigarette and beret. I sat down and we exchanged a few words and he praised my first book of poems. I hadn't yet met anyone from outside Kingston who had heard of the book, let alone read it, so I was startled and then happy to think that someone with a *nom de plume* and a beret could have any interest in what I wrote. It's not that I thought my work was bad — I didn't, most days — but I figured writers of the Queen Street set would find it too rustic, dull, remote from their own concerns. Later I would learn that Jones was interested in the full literary spectrum, not just in stuff that resembled or kept company with his own (as he proved through his eclectic editorial work with the journals *Open Letter* and, in the last two years of his life, with *Paragraph)* but at that moment his words of praise seemed to set up an unlikely bridge between worlds I had long thought exclusive — the private microcosm of my own lyrics and the larger demi-monde where poets sporting Kerouac tattoos and packets of Drum and Bad Attitudes wrote real poems, razor-edged and urban, and published them to the acclaim of the hip.

No doubt Jones — Daniel — would have laughed or smiled ironically if he'd known I considered him the Beat delegate of some realer world, some bohemian establishment.

We toasted each other on our new memberships and I left,
eager to get back up into the summer, and eager as well —
why not own up? — to escape and take a breather from the
very group I'd so much wished to join. Because now that I
did officially belong I was already claiming what any member
claims — the right to be both part and apart.

And now I wanted to drift home under old trees newly in
flower and to savour — in private — this sense of entry
and inclusion. Since things would be different from now
on. Right? Surely in future good work need not always be
"written in blood," through struggle, out of that strenuous
vein of solitude and longing where the truest art — deep
down we all know it — still pulses and flows. Yes, I lied to
myself. Why not. You can have it both ways. And suddenly
I could not wait to leave, as everybody else was doing, the
cash-bar closing, the house lights snapping on.

I took the stairs instead of the elevator and I took them two
at a time, feeling dizzy, drunk, reprieved; feeling somehow
as if I'd just gotten away with something. I left the stairwell
at what I took to be the lobby floor, two flights up. But I'd
climbed too far. I was in a residence hall. From somewhere
a sound of strummed guitars and frantic animation, laughter
flaring up and fading, flaring up again. For a minute or two
I stood there. The elevator door a few steps from me sprang
open and disgorged three women carolling in a drunk, but
decent, harmony: *Sweet dreams are made of this.* They linked
arms and swaggered three abreast up the hall, veering right
through an open door from which light and smoke and a
cheerful uproar flowed.

I walked back towards the stairwell and opened the fire
door. A man and woman now sat on the top stair, their backs
to me, heads tilted together. They stiffened and stopped
whispering but did not turn around. I backed out of the

stairwell and got into the elevator. Jabbed at the panel. The machine gave a weak metallic wheezing and started down. Drunk and Byronically lonesome, sentimental, I could now inflate myself into a lyrical visionary: The Poet foregoing the social amenities, to descend boldly, once again, into the depths.

The elevator decelerated with a sobering jerk, the doors clanked open, I walked out into darkness. I'd missed it again. Wrong floor. I was back in the basement. The house lights were now off and the dark was eased only by a weak, sullen light leaking in from the stairwells and the feeble slow-burn of exit signs. In that eerie glow, dozens of collapsible round tables could be seen cluttered with plastic cups, the floor littered with butts and pamphlets and paper napkins. And at the heart of this frat-house wreckage, slumped on a chair, feet propped side by side on a facing chair amid a clique of other chairs, all empty, Jones. A hand loosely tending the cup balanced on his groin. The other hand bringing a cigarette to his mouth. That same beret, so that even from where I stood in the near-dark, I knew him.

The steel doors shut behind me with a single metallic clap. I made my way among the tables and chairs. The floor under my boots was sticky. Daniel's face, pale and lunar, turned slowly towards me. When I reached him I did not sit down — afraid, I think, that pulling up a chair would have consummated my intrusion, finalized it, while standing here beside him I could still maintain the pretence that I was just passing through, on my way to that exit sign beyond him, the fire-door hidden in shadow beneath. Not meaning to cut in. Jones was the real writer. He was communing with his Muse in the basement crucible of the subconscious, spurning the wine-and-cheese chatter — he was not stricken with the need for approval, with the lostness, with the disaffiliation and manic mood-swings of the novice, since there must be some psychic turnstile or exit you pass through once and for all and finally escape all that shit. There must be, we have to believe that, and after all it turns out there is such a gate, though hardly the Arc de triomphe we imagined. He imagined. *By his own hand.*

I asked him how it was going. He looked up and lifted his cup a few inches. With the beret pushed way back on his high forehead and his pale eyes upturned, cigarette drooping from his lips, he looked doleful, bone-weary, a French resistance fighter in some old black-and-white film, brooding after a costly encounter with the enemy. But then he smiled. And gave a rich, sustained chuckle, not from the throat but deeper down, as if my banal inadequate query had been a dazzling witticism, dense with life-wisdom.

"I'm fine," he said. I think he did. Something like that.

"Just unwinding," I supplied, inanely.

He chuckled again. "It was a good party," he said. "My first time at the Union."

"Mine too."

"So you said."

"It's good to be a part of it."

He proffered his plastic cup. There was hardly anything left in it and I told him I couldn't drink any more anyway. I didn't know that he had quit drinking a few years before and that his cup must have held cola or soda water.

"Smoke?"

"No thanks."

He tossed his butt into the cup and lit a fresh one.

"It's cool down here."

"I hope I'm not intruding," I said. "Sometimes at parties, you know, I just go outside and sit there on my own. So I . . ."

"Not at all." He chuckled again. "I do too."

"Really?"

"Oh yes. I do the same. If I go to them."

Close, but no. Not quite. And maybe not so close after all. A few words, the general mood, how he looked up at me with damp, bloodshot eyes dully illumined by the light of the stairwells and his cigarette; my sense of transgression and inanity; my mounting concern; and, bound up with the compassion, a kind of predatory, professional curiosity. Yes. I remember those things, but few of the actual words. His words. Over the next few years I was to read his words in depth — in letters, stories, poems, a novel — but I was not to hear any more, not face to face, and at that moment I failed to listen with fully wakened ears. So now to resuscitate that last real-time meeting of ours I struggle like some translator of Sappho, piecing together a lyric out of smatterings, shards, and marginalia, determined to give the poet the last word.

I do know that after I shook his hand and turned away in the dead air and darkness of the basement, I moved with a kind of studied nonchalance towards the far fire-door, then hurried up a flight of stairs and burst out into the carnal heat and laden, fragrant air of a midsummer night, the sky a black net straining under its cargo of stars, the Milky Way so solid with light it was hard to believe its many suns were surging off from each other at unthinkable speeds. And Daniel? He was humming to himself softly as I passed through the door. I let the door close on that sound. I think now that when a lid folds down over a gone, beloved face, when the box closes like the cover of a finished book and the book gets filed away, a new kind of reading — a new kind of listening — begins. In the end the poets do become their best songs, and though most of their words are lost, the last word is always theirs, because it's song we turn to in time of storm and deepest need, when poetry is the one kind of speech that will do. And so it is here, Jones. Daniel. The last words are your own. *They were very good songs. I hear them still.*


*Spadina Hotel, Toronto, June 1995*

*Kingston, February 1996*

IN MEMORIAM D.J. (1959–1994)

# 13

# Still Possible to Be Haunted

*Religion and Writing in the Age of Career*

'*So tell me. . . . why were there so many great Catholic
composers in England?*' *None of us had an answer.* '*It's all
in the cadence. The line of beauty. The Catholics get it from
birth, in the rhythms of our Latin mass and benediction.*'
— Peter Ackroyd, *English Music*

*Writing is not an occupation.*
— Jay Ruzesky

I

ART BEGAN AS RELIGION and art is still religious, always —
even the most "secular" art, the most scatological, profane,
the most rational or "anti-religious" — because art in its
own way is always tied up with the staple questions, the
elemental mysteries that all religions start with and always
struggle to explore and explain. And of all the arts, literature
is the one most intimately linked to religion — "religion"
not as specific creed, or institution, but as all-embracing
perspective. This world-perspective is one I think of as

unitive, inclusive, and connectional, as set against the necessarily divisive, atomistic, and taxonomical perspectives of
science and secular philosophy. The religious spirit — as
opposed to the theological systems, rulebooks, and hierarchies that always encrust it and weigh it down — is what
unifies, not what codifies and fragments. In fact the word
religion is derived from the Latin *religare*, meaning to bind
or tie together.

I began to think about the connections that link literature
and religion on first noticing how a hugely disproportionate
number of the writers I knew, or knew of, had ministers or
priests for parents, or grandparents. And I saw that in a sense
I was one of them. Not that either my father or mother
was ever ordained. But in his teaching of high school and
university English my father's approach was always one of
inspired evangelism, while in the decade before his retire-
ment he became a regular reader of scriptural passages at the
church he'd begun to attend once more after a thirty-year
absence. It was as if, having obeyed a first calling as a teacher,
he was now being called a second time. Or had the teaching
always been a secular substitute for some deeper, priestly
vocation? I doubt that. As a teacher he was always much in
demand, and, as I heard later from ex-students and col-
leagues, a natural. One of my keenest regrets is that I never
got to see him teach.

Is it significant that I began to write "see him preach," then
caught myself? I think it is. Vocations do overlap. And if it's
true that the pedagogical and preacherly callings are closely
linked, it's even truer of the preacherly and the bookish.

But before saying anything more about the connection, let
me make it clear that I have no particular doctrinal axe to
grind. I'm a reader of all scriptures, a student of all creeds,
and an apologist for none. If I read the Bible, the Koran, the

*Tao The Ching*, the *Upanishads*, or Ojibway creation tales it's not owing to any sense of piety or to the beaverly enthusiasms of a pedant, but because of an ardent and abiding curiosity. If I visit holy sites and sit alone in mosques or old synagogues or Shinto shrines, it's not out of submission to the prescriptions of, say, Yahweh's prophets, or in order to make anthropological field notes, but because I sense in such places the gathered echoes of human ritual and longing — of that perennial search for meaning in which writers, in their own way, are also engaged. In the end it's the unitive and harmonic insights of the Buddha that seem to me the wisest — not to mention the truest ontologically, especially in light of findings this century in atomic and quantum physics — yet surely it's the story of Christ's passion that best embodies the drama and tragedy of human life as it's actually *lived*. Especially here in the West. The West whose restive, Faustian spirit of nonstop advance has infected the East as well, while its mania for ceaseless growth continues to contaminate every sea and landmass. . . . Christ is the tragically divided human consciousness, hung on the cross and torn apart between a heaven of mental abstractions and an earth of concrete physical desires — the garden of the senses, which also becomes, in the end, our grave. Meanwhile the Buddha — the spirit of the East — who passed through a stage of aery asceticism and fleshly denial before finally "touching earth" in his hour of enlightenment, represents the possibility of a different, less divided life, a doorway back into the garden.

Literature — even the most secular and seemingly offhand — is likewise a search for that opening in the wall.

## Staple Questions

It's hardly surprising that people exposed to religion in childhood should be overrepresented among adult writers. To start with, they grew accustomed early to the Big Questions so that in high school English when their teacher, eyeing his slack-jawed or gum-cracking flock, ironically declaimed "What a piece of work is man!" they knew it as an echo of earlier assertions, earlier questions — something of a kind they'd been hearing since childhood and whose incremental continuity added relevance, resonance, to their own hard questions. Who am I? And why am I here? The excruciating, eternal clichés.

The truth is that the religious sensibility — in the specific form of deep metaphysical curiosity, a need for meaning — is alive in even the "toughest" or most technolobotomized young person. In grade eight Debating we were asked to argue the existence or nonexistence of God and everyone had a strong opinion one way or another, just as we all had positions on the secular standbys of abortion and capital punishment. Even Barty Demenski — a drawling, horking, mouth-breathing cartoon of a bully who could bench-press (they said) five times his own IQ, who would sit on East Indian kids new to the school and regale them with "Paki jokes" then head-butt them if they failed to laugh, and who later became notorious for burying a cat to its neck in the earth and running a lawn mower over it — even Barty Demenski had something to share. Barty Demenski held that God could not possibly exist because his best friend's parents had just divorced and besides that he had another friend whose old man had just left home. (Everyone knew that Barty had at most one friend in the world, so in the second case he must have been talking about his own father.)

## *Mystery*

Though all religions offer prescriptive or at least tentative answers to the final questions, there remains at the heart of any religion — even the most definitive ones, like Islam — an abiding mystery. The face of God, the true name of God, that can never quite be glimpsed or uttered. A secret concealed in the tabernacle. It's in the context of organized religion that many artists as children first encounter that sense of impenetrable, irreducible mystery which, transposed into art, gives a poem or a sketch or a score its lasting, nagging power.

When I was five years old our family moved from Northern Ontario, where my father had found his first teaching job, to Toronto. And because at that time my Greek-Canadian mother was the only parent keen on organized religion, and there were a number of Greek Orthodox churches in the city, we began, for the first time, to go. My childhood exposure to church, clergy, scripture, and even Sunday school offered an unlimited experience of mind-scrambling mystery. I had seen Byzantine icons before, in the houses of Greek relatives, but never in such lavish abundance, and underlit by tiny, ranked choirs of candles, and hazed, like the upper air of the church itself, by marbled clouds of frankincense. The priest's cassock, hair, huge beard, and high brimless stovepipe hat were all as black as the long grieving-gowns of the widows who could be seen hunched or kneeling in every pew. How their veiled features — like coffined faces under shrouds of ebony mesh — unsettled me. And how the priest himself frightened me, towering past as he ushered the slow, solemn procession up the aisle during the Eucharist and his filigreed censer swung back and forth in a fog of fragrant myrrh like a blazing pendulum in the Book of the Apocalypse. The smell of the incense was sweet and foreign and made me think of funerals. The priest intoning and repeating phrases in a language I did not know — an old language, my mother would explain in a grave whisper, and one that even she could not translate. I came to learn certain cadences phonetically and to whisper them to myself, as all children repeat and incorporate new words. *Kirie Eleison. Thanatos, thanatos.* And when I grew bored during the long services I would look up and watch sunlit smatterings of incense snaking among rafters, and sometimes as I craned my head back to focus on that ribbed, vaulted ceiling I had the dizzying illusion of peering down into the hull of some vast wooden ship, as when the night sky above you seems like a chasm below, or like an ocean where multitudinous candles flicker and bob.

Of course much of the time I writhed with impatience and saw church as something that kept me from road hockey or *Hogan's Heroes* or *The Lord of the Rings*, but that sense of mystery that seized me at special times has never let go, and occasionally I'm still gripped by a desire to attend a service — Roman Catholic, Greek Orthodox, Anglican, the ones that haven't gutted the proceedings of all their mystery and ritual — or backwoods Baptist, where it's still all right to make a joyous noise unto the Lord, the way all religions briefly do before aging and stiffening into institutionhood. Then again, the Catholic and Orthodox churches have pretty much changed over to the vernacular, and though I grasp the democratic rationale for the change, I would surely be let down if I returned to the smouldering, capsized galleon of the church I sat in as a boy and could understand all the words — the lingering music of that first, foreign poetry.

## *Moral Resonance*

Literature, as opposed to schlock or simple reportage, resonates on a moral plane. This statement is not a prescription but an observation. The moral resonance I'm thinking of consists chiefly in the way that literature both uncovers and creates meaning. Fiction, for example, is inextricably bound up with what Hindu and Buddhist thought call the Law of Karma, the law of moral cause and effect, of consequentiality; everything that happens has its source in the past and whatever we do has its sequel in the future. So that everything we do has meaning, in the sense of resonance and implication. Good fiction (and sometimes bad) explores this truth and reminds us of it.

Again, it's not surprising that people with "religious backgrounds" are overrepresented among writers. Whether the writer has internalized Hindu ideas of karma or the Judeo-Christian sense of historical consequentiality, he or she is aware that life, and art, exist within a sweeping, cosmic context, and that the moral resonance without which fiction is just anthropology is contingent on time. Moral resonance is the echo an action makes in time; good art does not dogmatically indicate what's "right" or "wrong" but rather shapes the echo chamber within which actions can be heard to ring true or false, beautiful or evil, in key with life and growth or with death and stasis. (Needless to say most religions are far more definitive and dogmatic about right and wrong, good and evil — which is why it's usually the children of ministers who become poets, not the ministers themselves. Because the children were exposed to religion, absorbed it and then rebelled against it as they had to rebel against whatever their parents were; because the children took in the spirit and then burned the rulebook at the chapel door.)

But now more than ever it's possible to have an utterly secular childhood and never encounter Christian tenets of compassionate reciprocity or Confucian ideals of moral obligation. I'm no proponent of prayer in the schools — in fact I think the practice makes children view religion as a kind of punctual scholastic duty, like times-tables, or as some bloodless social form — but I do believe that unless you're exposed in childhood to some kind of transcendent mystery, even in the Romantic or New Age forms of nature or the night sky, the codes and platitudes of secular morality will carry no living weight. A child taught in a secular context that causing needless pain is wrong will "learn" the injunction in the same way one picks up an algebraic formula or a dollop of practical advice — mechanically and superficially. Another child, told the same thing while being encouraged to explore the fields of art, or of nature, or, say, human history — someone instilled with a sense of reverence for the magnitude of life — will come to grasp and take to heart the essential reason it's wrong to cause needless pain. (It's wrong because everything is connected.) The crimes of a Paul Bernardo do not represent the triumph of evil and the failure of reason so much as they headline the ascendancy of nihilism and abstraction. Which is to say, the failure of reverence. Of *perspective*. The serial killer knows in theory, in the abstract, that his actions are wrong, but only a sense of perspective, of reverence for life and the life force can make such knowledge an essential, cellular thing. Telling a child something without providing a radical, passionate context is like making a bully like Barty Demenski scribble some perfectly reasonable vow on the blackboard two hundred times. I WILL NOT CAUSE UNNECESSARY PAIN TO CATS. I WILL NOT CAUSE . . .

The roots of the late twentieth-century anomie that gets so much press these days is this lack of context. It's not a matter of taking your children back to church; I have no intention of doing that with my own. It is a matter of offering them more than a high-tech compass, a computer-graphic map, and a cranky inflexible rulebook (JUST SAY NO!) as aids to navigating a more and more intricate lifescape.

Art not only grows out of that passionate context — that subsoil of wonder — but helps to enrich and spread it. In other words art is not only religious, it serves a religious function. As for me, the books I devoured through grade school and high school (especially Albert Camus's *L'Étranger*, Arthur Koestler's *Darkness at Noon*, and J. D. Salinger's *The Catcher in the Rye*) were far more important in providing a layered moral subsoil than was my "religious background," which, if it comes to that, was relatively peripheral. But I see it all as part of the same vital context.

## Ritual, Tradition

I mentioned before how the rich unfamiliarity of the Greek Orthodox Church was, for me, a kind of agitation and inspiration. (Or to use the critical terminology of Russian Formalist Victor Schlovsky, it was a weekly *ostrenenie*, or defamiliarization, a kind of ontological wake-up call.) But I think the mass and the atmosphere of the church had a further helpful effect, as it has for so many writers with religion in their backgrounds — that of instilling a sense of ritual and tradition.

Children are deeply conservative and cherish ritual and tradition, as any parent knows who tries to alter a routine or change the ending of a story a child keeps asking to hear at bedtime. Most children as they grow into teenagers turn disdainfully from the routines and rituals of their parents and society, as they have to (as society needs them to, every rebellious generation serving as a kind of corrective that prevents social forms from calcifying as they otherwise will; hence the staleness and aesthetic sterility of societies where the young are too much in step with their parents, like postwar, pre-Beat, pre-rock-and-roll America). But while youthful rebellion is a needful and creative force, it amounts to nothing unless the young have a solid foundation of ritual and tradition to leap off from, to reject — something stable and solid to push off against. Without that, they go nowhere, are left flailing in a kind of ethical vacuum or void, forever nostalgic for childhood rituals they never fully had, too often apt to form life-or-death bonds with any surrogate or "virtual" family that can offer new rituals — whether of cult worship, group binges, or gang violence.

This is the predicament of more and more people today and for a young writer such lack of ritual context is a severe handicap. But what about those writers lucky enough to grow up with a sense of that continuum tying them to the past and thus rooting them in the present? Exposure to a religious tradition, as with Margaret Avison, or to a natural tradition, as in Christopher Dewdney's engaged knowledge of geological history, gives poetry (say) a kind of layered substratum of deeper awareness, an historical context, an echoing resonance without which a poem is just verse, a story just anecdote, a novel sociology. The difference between reading I-do-this-and-feel-that-and-all-in-the-present-tense workshop verse and the layered poetry of P. K. Page or Al Purdy is like the difference between hearing Aerosmith on a cheap tinny AM radio and Tom Waits or The Clash on a good stereo: depth and resonance. The sound of history echoing in the present and shooting it through with meaning.

## *Time*

The millenarian, directional nature of Judaistic, Islamic, and Christian thought is so fundamental to the Western world-view that it's hard to say if the writing of those with religious backgrounds really differs, in terms of narrative trajectory, from the writing of those without. But whether directly or indirectly, the apocalyptic, historical religions — those that move teleologically — have had an enormous effect on the shape of Western literature, imposing a consistent linearity and forward thrust, a sense that crises of reckoning and revelation are close at hand. A Second Coming, as in the poetry of Yeats; a day of judgement, as in the stories of Flannery O'Connor; an arrival at epiphany, as in the stories of James Joyce, that "apostate Catholic" (as David Lodge calls him), "for whom the writer's vocation was a kind of profane priesthood." On the other hand the more circular, cyclical traditions of Buddhism, Hinduism, Shintoism, animism, and Native American thought have been affecting narrative shape more and more this century as West and East, North and South, increasingly interconnect. Western novelists writing of the East, like Joseph Conrad, or writing in the Magic Realist tradition, like Gabriel García Márquez and Günter Grass, show the influence of non-Western temporal conceptions; and while Western poetic forms like the epic and the sonnet are both supremely directional — the epic being a narrative in verse while the lines of the sonnet always press on towards the revelation of its closing couplet — the epic has almost disappeared, while the lyric free verse that has replaced it has shown a very Eastern concern with timeless, undirectional imagery, and with ambiguity instead of revelation.

## Suffering

The first principle or Great Truth of Buddhism is that all living things suffer, while Christianity, as Oakland Ross has pointed out, is based on the life and death of a torture victim. The Byzantine icons that I first saw as a child were especially graphic and gruesome, and though at the time I was morbidly fascinated by the baroque contortions of those sallow, skeletal Christs, the incremental effect, I think, was to deepen my awareness of suffering. I had a first inkling of this effect in my early teens when I saw Norman Jewison's 1973 film version of *Jesus Christ Superstar*. Just before the crucifixion and in time to one of the most dramatic riffs in Andrew Lloyd Webber's score, a sequence of crucifixion images flash one by one before the viewer's eyes like the slides of battered victims at a war crimes inquest or the trial of a serial killer. By the end of that grisly collage I was salting my popcorn with tears — an especially unwelcome activity for a teenaged guy, with friends, at a cinema. Andrew Lloyd Webber was an artist in those days.

Earlier I cited Roo Borson's idea of "radical compassion," using it to suggest the essentially religious life-reverence and empathy pervading almost all good art; it's a deep awareness of suffering you're far more likely to acquire in a (broadly) religious context than in secular terms. On TV and in video games countless villains are hurt or killed, sure, but their duplicate mechanical maimings are only a shade, a cartoon of real suffering.

## The Writer as Priest

The world is already too rife with evangelists and missionaries — religious, commercial, ideological — people whose fundamentalist quackery and propheteering is dangerous and repellent, and yet as with Joyce, the profane priest, it can hardly be denied there's an evangelist of a kind in every writer. The contemporary performance poet is obviously a kind of street preacher, but even the writer who never takes the show on the road is playing a kind of apostolic role. This is true whether it's Salinger offering us the skaz gospel of Holden Caulfield or John Irving showing us the world according to Garp, G. M. Hopkins writing elaborate hymns that rupture the sonnet form with the pressure of the preaching, Leon Rooke ranting over the page like some inspired revivalist, or Margaret Atwood, in *The Handmaid's Tale*, warning us about Moral Majoritarians and other Buchananites as if exposing the heresy of some rival sect.

Polemical essays, like those of Douglas Fetherling, John Metcalf, or Brian Fawcett, are more overtly sermonic and use all the characteristic modes and tropes of the sermon — anecdote, invective, extended metaphor, humour, incantation, the brimstone crescendo — but even the subtlest, most ambiguous and least definitive short story is a kind of moral address that seeks to convey some truth (though without making any simplistic point at the end, pious moralizing being the preserve of institutional religion and its "morality" chiefly in service of the status quo).

Religion — true religion — is interested not in moral pulpitry or codified laws but in the Law, the *Tao*, the Way.

## Magic in Language

Then finally the magic of words. The Word. Above all it's this connection between religion and art that is most manifest in literature, that makes literature the most religious of the arts. I wrote before about how in boyhood I was intrigued, and haunted, by phrases of hymn and scripture intoned by a towering priest in an ancient language I could never hope to understand. Yet this is also the experience of writers exposed to scriptural cadences in their own language — English, for example — because the archaic sonorities of the Book of Common Prayer and the King James Bible, and even of some recent translations, carry a weight and a mystery that work their way into the mind. *Thy will be done*, it says in The Lord's Prayer; I'm sure I wasn't the only child who could not quite understand what that phrase meant. Thy *what* be done? I knew the word *will* only as a verb, so that *thy*, it seemed, could only be a noun. But what could "thy" mean? Did it mean *you*, as it seemed? Or something else? And what was going to be done to whomever, or whatever? I would ponder such mysteries while I stood fidgeting at my desk at 8:55 a.m., thoughts of Dave Keon and the Maple Leafs scuttling through my mind and would I get the Leafs sweater I wanted for Christmas and what magical changes were happening to Lucia, the girl I was then "in love" with, her breasts first to bloom in the class and seemingly growing by the day? I would write poems for her and leave them in her desk. I seem to recall that the poems contained a lot of thys and thees, and that sometimes a day or two later I would find them in the garbage, scrunched or shredded and half hidden under other trash; I was never sure whether she did that out of discretion or disdain. But I kept writing poems and before long they were being inscribed to other girls — Amanda, Sandra, Kim. It never struck me as odd that the lucky target of my foolscap arrows could change that way without the tone and style of the poems changing too. Years later I would read Auden's warning to lovers: if there's one thing you can be sure of, it's that when someone is garreted away writing you a love poem, YOU are the last thing on his mind. Put another way, the subject of poetry is not just the person or thing that a poem's "about," or even the "emotions" of the poet, but language itself. Every lover on first trying to write a love poem instinctively knows that the exalted feeling driving him or her is somehow religious, and that the vernacular — the argot of weekdays, spreadsheets, and grocery lists — will never cut it. Eliot once noted that in moments of emotional crisis everyone speaks in poetry; another way to put it is to say that in moments of rapture, deep love, fury, or grief, all people speak in prayer.

Needless to say my poems for Lucia and Amanda and Sandra were just baroque embroideries of romantic clichés, Hallmark and CHUM top-forty platitudes, ludicrous pseudo-religious vows, but already I and the other crypto-poets in the school had learned something from the half-understood lines of prayer before morning announcements. In love, for a brief time, we make the beloved our religion and while the spell lasts we can see clearly how much of the language around us is moribund — bloodless, figureless, so much of its style and fire extinguished. Language filed down to an efficient machine, tooled for the accomplishment of practical secular ends; the dictionary reduced to a kind of operator's manual. And the rhythmically shambling, dusty punditry of academics and academies, and the evasive rhetoric of politicians, and the abstract unrelenting pamphletese of institutions and the rote recitations of burnt-out teachers and parents and the manic muppetry of talk-show hosts and admen — this is the way the world ends, not with a bang but to the râle of canned laughter.

The story goes that one time towards the end of his life Elvis was lounging with his retinue in Graceland, drugged up and watching some variety show on TV. Robert Goulet came on stage and started crooning, all style and no substance. After a minute or so Elvis pulled out a .45 revolver and blew the television to bits. A moment of near-silence, the jagged wreckage sizzling and fuming, a soft clinking as Elvis cleared the spent shells into his palm. After a minute or so one member of the retinue supposedly ventured, "Say, Elvis, why did you do that?"

"Because," Elvis said, "he didn't mean it."

These days I think more and more about the importance of belief — of really meaning it — in art. I think about charged and layered language, the language of poets like Hopkins and Dickinson, Lynn Crosbie and Michael Redhill and Don McKay, whose words speak to us of a reality beyond the spreadsheet and the stock market, a place where "the Holy Ghost broods over the bent / World with warm breast and with Ah! Bright wings." It doesn't matter at all if the writer believes in a personal god, or in any god, or in the "Holy Ghost" that Hopkins did most emphatically believe in; every writer is haunted by a holy ghost. By which I mean: an abiding sense of wonder, of life-reverence, of "radical compassion." And as the religious sensibility disappears from a more and more technogogic world, and from the realm of writing, it leaves the writer himself or herself a ghost of a different kind — not warm-breasted and visionary, but a rootless spectre, unable to bear meaningful witness to the things that must be seen, and said.

The haunted writer is always an apostle for the heart.

2

*In the context of our unstable times, people are encouraged to regard themselves as a kind of product, one that has to be marketed effectively on an ongoing basis.*
— Diane Lefebvre

*That's me in the spotlight, losing my religion.*
— Michael Stipe

IF IT'S TRUE that the best writers are essentially religious, how are they to keep the faith nowadays, and remain, in the broadest sense of the word, believers? Again I have to stress what I'm not suggesting: that you or I must believe in something specific, like Jehovah or Allah or Ogun, or in papal infallibility, or in the inspired authority of the church. In this connection it's worth noting how T. S. Eliot's poetic powers declined as his piety and obeisance to the Anglo-Catholic Church — to laws and dogma instead of the spirit of love it all began with — increased in shrillness and stiffness. *Four Quartets* lays down the law; *Prufrock* pulses with the spirit. *Prufrock* remains Eliot's most radically religious poem. And his best.

But if Eliot's powers were gradually diminished by his embrace of limiting theological dogmas — his loss, that is, of Keats's "negative capability" — writers today risk corruption by another force, a force which in Eliot's time was not nearly so strong as it is now. I mean the pressure that writers, along with everyone else, feel to commodify and incorporate themselves like growing businesses; to produce at the highest possible rate and to sell to the highest bidder; to be good secular citizens in the Age of Career. The crux of the problem is this: to survive as a full-time writer you have to manage your affairs in a way that is partly salesmanlike and careerist, while to keep on writing serious work, relevant work — to remain an artist — you have to maintain or deepen a vocational, sacramental connection to your work. Or to your soul — that part of you that is you alone and has been from the first, that is not just a social construct (though much of you plainly is), that speaks to you sometimes in the night and not just in the argot of the media and the marketplace but in the lyrical cinema of dream.

And this immediate, undistracted connection — this religious integrity of worker and work — has to be maintained despite the growing distractions and mediations of modern, high-speed, careerist life.

There never has been a Golden Age for writers and in many ways the lives of writers, as of people in other crafts and trades, were harder fifty or a hundred years back. Still, those of George Gissing's or F. Scott Fitzgerald's generation did know that a niche in the culture was reserved for them — that with luck they could make what Kent Nussey has called "a civilized pact with the world" — while now, it seems, writers do not make pacts so much as they submit and surrender to something larger than themselves, the market, Mammon, a power that functions like a machine. If they don't want to disappear, that is. And the "lucky" ones, who manage not to be disappeared under the incurious, oblivious bulk of the corporate machine, are soon drawn into the works of another, connected mechanism, the star-maker modem, whose circuitry grows more efficient all the time and always ends up distorting the product it grinds out. Laser printing or no. A NEW STAR.

Distorting or destroying it.

So how is one to balance a calling, a career?

This is the age of the career. Career and its threat to "calling" are not new things, but their universality is new, and now the classic career arc or trajectory — of a steady unsevered rise towards some sort of personal and professional climax — is as deeply grooved into our thought circuits as was the "line of rising action" for students of the short story back when I was in school. Seeing as that pattern (of rising action, climax, and dénouement, or of rising action and epiphany) still works best for many stories, and no doubt always will; seeing as it's been around as long as civilization (but has now been democratized); and seeing as it follows the arc of some of life's most basic and engaging narratives (the chase, the love affair, the argument, the orgasm), it is tempting to see it as somehow organic, natural, a law of human nature and of life itself. But as Linda Rogers has pointed out, the orgasm of uninterrupted rising action is not the only kind, is perhaps more typically male, and while it is supremely organic, it's not nature's only arc. Yet proponents of "selfish gene" theories go on arguing that the need for "career" in the modern sense is organic, is natural to humanity — the rising line of ambition an accurate graph of human self-interest. I don't know. Ambition is natural enough — a form of the necessary impulse to secure power of some kind, to survive — but there's nothing "naturally human" about the stereotyped course it's now meant to follow. As if the careering of a saddled, jockeyed horse bursting out of a steel starting pen then spurred and whipped around a manmade track is naturally equine.

And the word "career"? It's interesting to consider how most of the world's languages lack any indigenous equivalent to "career" in our more current sense of one's climb up the ladder of professional life. Destiny and fate, for which there are equivalents in every tongue, hardly mean the same thing.

Nor are they words much in use now anyway. Poets, though, might be better off — poetically if not professionally — viewing their work in terms of destiny and fate, not career, and taking to heart the credo of the classical tragedians: Character is fate. Because if time is seen as a kind of trellis over which a life grows, then one's work and character are like vines, intertwined, growing upward together and then in maturity arcing down again to re-enter the soil. Like the Buddha touching earth in his hour of enlightenment; like Rilke in the *Duino Elegies* crying out, to Nature, "You were always right."

In the course of a career something very different happens. Career uproots the character and catapults it upward too fast and too far.

The fast track of career differs from the slow road of fate the way a flight path differs from a forest trail.*

In a careerist age even artists of a highly private and patient temperament find that the ubiquitous and sanctified idol of Career has found its way inside them, like a moneylender into the temple. In her essay "Diary of a Loser" Sharon Butala gives a vivid picture of what can happen to a writer suddenly saddled with a big career — how potently it can affect even those who have taken steps to exorcise or avoid possession by the contemporary, careerist Zeitgeist. Butala herself has taken the step of settling in an isolated pocket of the Prairies, but for a while that was not enough. In *Coyote's Morning Cry* she writes of how her previous book *The Perfection of the Morning* had been "about seven months, at

---

* To use a classical analogy, career traces the trajectory of Icarus (though not always to his fall), while the path of a serious artist should sometimes descend before rising again, like Orpheus. (Meanwhile the rent cheque is due and the phone bill wants paying.)

various times, on three Canadian bestseller lists (for a short period on all three at once) and had been number one on the most important list." She was a finalist for a number of awards, including the Governor General's Award, and in the late fall she was waiting for the results:

> I couldn't concentrate on my writing, or think seri-
> ously with any depth about anything, and, worst of all,
> I could no longer make a connection with Nature, no
> matter how hard I tried. . . . I could not . . . find any
> joy in the fields, the stone circles, the coyotes that
> seemed, unaccountably, to be haunting the place.

In the end the Governor General's Award went to some-body else, though Butala did win two other prizes for her book. Still, she felt the "losing" more than the "winning" and for a while after the excitement had died down (though the book remained a strong bestseller) she continued to feel distracted, detached from "Nature." Then finally there came a day when she "stood in the doorway of her office . . . and felt, for the first time in weeks, that deep stirring of calm and simple delight that meant . . . [she would] be able to write again."

Calm and simple delight. Any childhood lover of books remembers that wave of relief and exaltation that would buoy you the moment you realized you could return to a book you'd been living deep inside for days. So that you would climb back in, as into a cardboard-box fort, and close the cover behind you like a door. Such is one common encounter with what American essayist Sven Birkerts calls "deep time" — that clockless, borderless psychic state whose inhabitants have dual citizenship and can live out in the world with others, or deep in the collaborative, fantastic world of books.

Adults are not barred from that state, but it takes real time and peace to get to the border, and for adults such commodities are scarce. Birkerts argues further that the speed of our lives has accelerated to the point where even for children the experience of "deep time" grows rare.*

The religious sensibility from which all art springs is threatened whenever "deep time" is threatened. Books like *The Master and Margarita*, *Blood Meridian*, and *From the Fifteenth District* can only be written by citizens of some personal arrondissement in this ambit of "deep time." Because art, like the religious insights to which it's akin, springs from solitude and longing, and the careerist world makes a two-pronged attack on these things. First of all the creative solitude that writers must protect — and endure — can be eroded by proliferating social functions which have nothing to do with the sacramental compulsion of art, but are hard to resist for writers trying not to disappear, trying to "make it," trying to escape the exhausting company of their own minds. Meanwhile if a writer does start to succeed it becomes too easy for her to go out into the street and find flattering, distracting company instead of staying inside, at the desk, walled up in the garret of the skull.

Second, and following closely from the first, the writer's

---

* It could be argued that children immersed for hours in the virtual reality of video games are also experiencing a kind of "deep time," and I suppose they are, but it's not the same kind as the reader's "deep time" and I believe it's lesser coin. First, the reader's state involves imaginative and empathetic collaboration while the video-player's state involves, at best, a kind of mechanical collaboration. Second, when a reader returns from the timeless world of a book to "real time" it's often with a sense of leavened, "defamiliarized" perception; it's hard to imagine a game of Tetris or Super Mario heightening anything but one's sense of distance and alienation from the world.

necessary longing — good art being a marriage of craving and craft — can be blunted or otherwise bought off by the secular perks and consolations that come with success, praise filing the sharp edge off a writer's desire. As Charles Foran writes of the many rock stars who seem to have sold out, "What is routinely confused with surrendering to greed is more likely the gradual diminishment of those early compulsions." Then, too, if the writer's career begins to move and he gets drawn out of the sacramental realm and fed into the secretarial mill, the harried, hyperkinetic rhythms of careerist tasks may come to accelerate his natural creative pace — and on the page it may alter the actual rhythm of his sentences — while the breezy wine-and-cheese schtick of the Smiling Public Man slowly accustoms him to glib, inauthentic discourse.

These factors can't fail to weigh together against the stirring of "calm and simple delight," the experience of "deep time" — and this if you're lucky enough to get a career in the first place. For those who are not noticed, the pace and price of things in the age of career make it tougher than ever to hang on without the small but steady income of royalties, readings, grants, and teaching stints — and in a world which shows itself at every turn a lover of worldly success, and increasingly crabby about impractical and unproductive things like "the humanities" and "callings," the lack of attention is more of an indignity than ever.

I still have no fax machine, but when the phone rings I often pick it up. Better a disruptive phone call than no word from outside. Only it's the phone company, or the Canadians for Capital Punishment Now, or a wrong number, etc., etc. They say the author of *Blood Meridian*, Cormac McCarthy, ripped his phone out by the roots twenty years ago. I wonder if that act seemed to him as dramatic, bizarre, and bold as it does to someone of my generation, reared not in a forest of symbols but a forest of signals.

If the great writers are the ones who focus most profoundly, and this age is one of increasing distractions, could it be that the age of great writing is gone? In his essay "Filling in the Millennium, a Primer in Belief and Technique," Kent Nussey writes of a daydream in which he heard a voice say to him, "In the future the only real writers will be the saints." But "sinners" might have done as well, at least in the eyes of the technoestablishment with its balance sheets and bottom lines, since the latter-day Luddites and Romantics and other grotesques will be defiantly "unproductive," uncooperative — the impractical eccentric ones who wind up in desert ghost towns or on abandoned farms with their families or in cheap inner-city rooms, maybe not cork-lined rooms like Proust's, but somehow out of touch and off-line. Anywhere it's still possible to be haunted.

Over the last year or two I've been thinking about career and calling because I now have a small career. I'm not a best-seller by any means, but the phone does ring. I know that the conflict between the vocational, the *sacramental* element of the writer's life and the unavoidable clerical part is as old as writing, but I also see how the manic, coked-up tempo of the careerist age intensifies the dilemma. Sometimes I wonder if writers like Wallace Stevens and T. S. Eliot had it right, working full-time for much of their lives in professions which, the poetic evidence suggests, paid back little by way of material, while making huge demands on their energy and time. Could be that Stevens, and definitely Eliot, were not cut out by temperament or upbringing for the bohemian life, and surely working with people does yield vital insights that can't be gleaned or deduced in an ivory solitude — but it may be more to the point that by working daily in a field separate from their art, Eliot and Stevens were never tempted to confuse a job for a calling, a calling for a job.*

What exactly does a literary career entail these days? Even if you're not a bestseller, careerist obligations can sometimes make you nostalgic for the days when nobody knew you but you had time enough to write, and all the solitude and longing in the world.

I decided to leave university after getting an MA in English Literature because I could see that the academic life was not for me and I was bored of grinding out essays. I wanted to write fiction and poetry, full-time if possible. But if the notorious necessity of having to write and publish essays "or perish" had soured me on the academic life, I soon learned that out in "the real world" the same went for novelists, poets, and aspiring bohemians of all stripes.

To have a career, it was said, you were supposed to publish a book a year. That was the cold, exacting calculus of literary survival. When I first heard someone cite this Calvinist timetable it bothered me only because it sounded like an impossibility. It still does. Gradually, though, I came to see

---

* No doubt it's best not to live so compartmentally, but in a world where the sacred and the profane are so thoroughly segregated, it's hard to live any other way. Buddhist ethics would urge that the clerical *is* sacramental, and surely Thich Nhat Hanh, the Buddhist monk and philosopher, is right to advise doing daily chores in a serene, meditative, and "mindful" way. But in the age of career the chores can multiply beyond all reasonable scope, and, as Thoreau pointed out in *Walden*, "a man's life will be spent." Or a woman's: Sylvia Plath carving out a career for herself in poetry while trying to manage a household — a different but equally difficult balancing act, work with children being more exhausting than other jobs and at the same time more rewarding in insight and inspiration.

that the trouble with applying the publish or perish equation to literature lay not so much in the finitude of physical energy, but in the limits of imaginative energy. And — to revert to my equation of writing with religion — to the limits of vision. It's one thing to build an academic career out of diligent, regular ratiocination, since abstract thought, being little bound by the body's organic limits, is constrained only by consciousness. It's a totally different thing to will a book of poems into being. Philip Larkin once remarked that he had "never [gone] looking" for his poems; the publish or vanish imperative means that many writers today feel obliged to beat the underbrush and hunker before dawn in chilly brakes with duck whistles and moose calls, when after all the best poems and stories are the ones that come hunting us, haunting us, with tigerlike stealth, to jump us when our guard is down.

Inspiration, aesthetic or religious, is always a form of ambush.

Another pressure I've felt along with countless others is the pressure to write a novel. These days the career arc of the "serious writer" involves a kind of corporate hierarchy where poetry — the original and densest, most difficult form — is on the ground floor in the janitor's storeroom, short stories a couple of flights up with the clerks and gofers, while the novel, stogey in hand, golf-shoes up on the desk, lords it in the penthouse. ("Non-fiction," as the negative cast of the term might lead you to expect, figures nowhere in this exclusive floor plan and need not apply.) Writers are to try their hand first at poetry or stories, then, after publishing a book or two, move onward and upward. Sadly this generic class system, which has less to do with intrinsic value than with the relative size of the genres (and, collaterally, their marketability), encourages writers to see poetry and short fiction as means to an end (the novel) instead of ends in themselves. . . . I've always wanted to write novels and I mean to, but lately I've been feeling a perverse itch to buck the career plan and write something perfectly unmarketable — like an epic poem in *terza rima*. About a goatherd. In Idaho. As if pushing on — onward and upward — to the penthouse would represent a kind of capitulation to the spirit of this careerist age, where everything is supposed to grow and climb and rise, World without End, Amen.* These days even poets, traditionally immune to market coercion because there is no real market, are feeling pressure from small publishers to submit unified collections of poems, neat packages which can be "marketed" more effectively than a random grouping. No use blaming the publishers for the pressure — they're only passing along a stress they're feeling themselves.

By demanding bigger books, or unified packages, the age and the world of career once again endorse product over process, the worldly over the sacramental.

And once the book has been willed into the going shape, and accepted, and published, it's time to take it on tour. I've come to like giving readings; these days I see them not only as a chance to introduce people to my own work in an unmediated form, but to try convincing the unconverted that fiction and poetry are living, dynamic, and necessary, not just good for you in some old-fashioned way. I've attended poetry readings whose feature acts put me in mind

---

* "They cannot see that growth for growth's sake is a cancerous madness. . . . They would never understand that an economic system which can only expand or expire must be false to all that is human" (Edward Abbey, on corporate capitalism, in *Desert Solitaire*).

of the mummified Jeremy Bentham, exhumed from cold storage annually for the meeting of the Board of Governors at University College, London, and propped in his chair for the duration. Readings from which certain members of the audience, attending a literary event for the first time (perhaps out of curiosity, perhaps because some people really are as mad as hell, sick of things virtual and craving exposure to the visceral and the real) fled in disorder and obvious disappointment. Never to return. I was a Benthamite when I started reading. I've worked hard to improve. I take as models poets like Patrick Friesen and P. K. Page and Erin Mouré — writers who could make an audience of the most jaded skeptics believe that poetry, like a sense of religious wonder, is still possible, still essential. That life is short and literature matters.

All the same, a schedule dense with public appearances has an undeniably depleting effect on a writer. Most writers I speak to will admit (as I will) to being dispositionally unfit for public appearances, photo ops and interviews and TV spots and reading tours. Actors and dancers and musicians, accustomed to performance, generally sweat less under the spotlight than do writers and painters (most of whom become artists partly from a fundamental shyness and whose introversion better equips them to explore inner worlds of memory and dream) — but the pressures of the media schmooze and the marketplace are unavoidably centrifugal and pull all artists apart, outward, away from the heart's true centre and the realm of "deep time."*

---

* "One problem afflicting a successful author these days is that he is almost paid and encouraged not to write and to spend all his time just talking to audiences" (Pico Iyer, interviewing Kazuo Ishiguro in *Harper's*, winter 1996).

There's a sense in which a writer needs to cultivate a kind of controlled agoraphobia. Maybe Walt Whitman didn't, but times have changed. It may be true that we've always maintained public and private selves that differ to some degree, but in this McLuhanesque epoch the divide keeps deepening and the wider it grows, the harder it gets to return, in silence and privacy, to the true self. And to the authentic things it has to say. Because the glib argot of the wine and cheese party or the stereotyped patter of the interview or the prating of the ego, in those fleeting times when you begin to credit the hyperbole of your best reviews, are all forms of dead language. I doubt I'm the only writer who has found that when the readings are over it can take a while — too long — to tune in again to the right inner station and get back to writing in a clear voice. Or, in Sharon Butala's terms, to hear the cries of the coyotes unaccountably gathered on the rangeland.

Those quiet voices are easily overwhelmed by that Zen conception, "the drunken monkey that prattles" — by the voice of the ego, its caffeinated chatter drowning out the whisperings of the soul. Even in the night, when the ego is meant to sleep, so the place you dream in is diminished to a dusty coop chittering with sterile anxieties instead of widening with time into a forest rich with totems, ghosts, and portents. As for the day, when artists need to maintain or cultivate the capacity to dream while awake, the management of a career demands the unsleeping vigilance of the ego, which like a noon sun or a blazing set of spotlights blinds the eye and scatters the fragile hints and figments of revery.

So how is one to protect the creative spirit against the effects — secretarializing or self-conscious-making — of career? Whether a small career is making you feel and function like a clerk, or a big career like a king, in secular terms you've been promoted and your art now lives on a lower floor. . . .

The tour ends and you go home, half hoping the phone will be ringing off the hook and at the same time craving the peace and anonymity from which new work might come. There may be reviews waiting for you — that is, if you're lucky, and writing fiction, and those tumouring newspaper chains haven't bottomlined serious reviews out of existence; and if there are reviews, you're back on the rollercoaster the ego rides when a book is just out. So to keep those centrifugal pressures from sucking all the creative goods from your core, you grow a thick tough hide, like everyone else, and then you're ready as well for the scathing reviews and the rejection slips. Yet you know that to write your best you have to be thin-skinned too — porous, permeable, wide open to nature and human life, taking everything in. Unbudgeably arrogant — so you can handle the hard knocks — yet humble as a desert beggar with his bowl.

I felt full of myself after my first good reviews. The feeling did encourage me to write more, but two-thirds of the book I wrote under the influence of that secular inspiration was willed and inauthentic, every false poem a kind of faked orgasm. For a few weeks — and at odd times since — I've enjoyed that feeling of power that even the smallest success can excite. Now I can see that power and poetry can't cohabit any more than power and authentic religious feeling can coexist. The ambitious cardinal has long since lost touch with his god, and any poet of worldly power (Leonard Cohen, Maya Angelou, Yevgeny Yevtushenko, Seamus Heaney, Derek Walcott, a handful of others) who continues to produce good work does so only to the extent that he or she finds ways to deflate the natural burgeoning of the ego, to cure the cancer before it metastasizes and spreads to the soul.

Once I sat and tried to meditate for an hour on a snide review. The idea, of course, was to put this infinitesimal setback into a cosmic perspective, to remind myself that suffering begets suffering, that the reviewer may have been sarcastic out of his own pain and disappointment. To remind myself that, as Norman Levine has said, "nothing matters but the work." To this lofty end I strove to focus a mind suffused with compassion on every point, every phrase, every word of the review.

By the end of the session I'd sworn to track the reviewer down and shoot him.

(I try now not to focus on either the bad or the good.)


Writers born and raised in the age of the career feel compelled to wrestle anxieties before they wrestle the angel, if they ever do. Don't get me wrong, I do want to have a career of some kind, I've seen the desolation of good writers who get passed over somehow and I know where that can lead; as the German phrase has it, "Despair does not write at all." At the same time I've stopped doubting that career can turn what should be a kind of pilgrimage into a crazed, cut-throat rodeo in which you may cross the finish line first — a success in the world's eyes — but diminished.

The Talmud teaches that "Every blade of grass has its Angel that bends over it and whispers, 'Grow! Grow!'" — but the blade grows only so far and to its own measure and with the sense to rise and then go fallow, then shoot back up, in step with the season's silent decrees. Maybe Kent Nussey is right and in the future the only real writers will be the saints — the ones willing to chase the moneylenders from the temple, the ones who find a way to keep the space around them holy. Nothing could be harder than that, not now.

# Acknowledgements

MOST OF THE ESSAYS in *The Admen Move on Lhasa* were written in Kingston between 1988 and 1996. During that time a number of people helped me by reading the essays in draft form, by talking and arguing with me about some of the ideas, and by commissioning some of the essays in the first place.

As always, heartfelt thanks and love to Mary Huggard, first reader and last; to Martha Sharpe, my patient and generous editor at Anansi; and to Ken Babstock, Colin Boyd, Mark Cochrane, Mary Cameron, Tom Carpenter, Eric Folsom, Wayne Grady, Jenny Haysom, John and Lambie Heighton, Jason Heroux, Michael Holmes, Jake Klisivitch, Jane Lafarga, Anne McDermid, Peter McPhee, John Metcalf (as always), Chris Minor, Kent Nussey, Joanne Page, Richard Outram, Michael Redhill, Neil Reynolds, Oakland Ross, Jay Ruzesky, Julian Scala, Harvey Schachter, Merilyn Simonds, Mark "The Knife" Sinnett, Carolyn Smart, David Staines, and Derk Wynand. A special thank you to the editors of *Brick* — Linda Spalding, Esta Spalding, and Michael Ondaatje — who published three of the essays.

Thanks also to the Canada Council and the Ontario Arts Council, whose support at key times was a great help.

The author is grateful to the editors and organizers of the following magazines and workshops, where earlier versions of the essays were published or presented: *Brick* ("The Admen Move on Lhasa," "Training for the Millennium," and "Apollo VI and the Flight from Emotion"), *Freelance*, and the Writers' Guild of Saskatchewan AGM, Moose Jaw, April 1994 ("In the Suburbs of the Heart"), *The Malahat Review* ("The Age of Clowns"), *The New Quarterly* ("Still Possible to Be Haunted"), *Pottersfield Portfolio* ("Deaths and Entrances"), *Prairie Fire*, and The Manitoba Writers' Guild AGM, Winnipeg, September 1994 ("The Electrocution of the World"), *Quill & Quire* ("Firing Line"), *This Country Canada* and *Quarry Magazine* ("Elegy in Stone"), *The Whig-Standard Magazine* ("Firing Line" and "A Wild Peculiar Joy"), The Maritime Writers' Workshop, Fredericton, July 1995 ("The Admen Move on Lhasa").